HOW TO DO just about ANYTHING IN

Microsoft®

Word

READER'S DIGEST

HOW TO DO just about ANYTHING IN

Microsoft®

Word

Published by The Reader's Digest Association Limited
London • New York • Sydney • Montreal

For Reader's Digest

Editor
Caroline Boucher

Art Editor
Conorde Clarke

Sub-editor
Rachel Weaver

Technical Consultant
Tony Rilett

Proofreader
Barry Gage

Index
Marie Lorimer

Reader's Digest General Books

Editorial Director
Julian Browne

Art Director
Anne-Marie Bulat

Head of Book Development
Sarah Bloxham

Managing Editor
Nina Hathway

Picture Resource Manager
Sarah Stewart-Richardson

Pre-press Account Manager
Penelope Grose

Production Controller
Sandra Fuller

Product Production Manager
Claudette Bramble

How to do just about anything in Microsoft® Word - Office 2007 is based on previous editions of this book which were edited, designed and produced by:

Planet Three Publishing Network
Northburgh House,
10 Northburgh Street,
London EC1V 0AT

Acknowledgments

We would like to thank the following individuals and organisations for their assistance in producing this book.

Photography: Karl Adamson
Equipment: Dell Computer Corporation

Contents

Basics

Styling Your Text

Styling Your Document

Editing Text

Customising Word

Using Graphics

Special Functions

How to use this book

This book is a fun and approachable guide to mastering Microsoft Word. All the most useful features of the program are clearly set out as step-by-step projects, with pictures that show you exactly what you will see on screen. Unlike a manual, you'll never find yourself wondering how to complete a task or having to unravel complicated instructions.

GETTING AROUND THE BOOK

This book covers the main features of Word. You can either read it from start to finish, or dip in and out, as you wish.

Basics
Are you completely new to Word? Learn how to create, save and print your first ever document.

Customising Word
Word's automatic settings dictate how you work. Find out how to set your own preferences.

Styling text
You can style text to suit all kinds of documents, from formal letters to party invitations. Discover the typefaces and how to size and style them.

Styling your document
Word is an extremely versatile program. Learn how to make your newsletter look professional,

use columns of text, set indents on paragraphs, create stylish borders and lots more.

Editing text
With just a few key strokes, you can select and move whole paragraphs of text, and search for and replace words or phrases. Thanks to Word's spellchecker and thesaurus, you can also ensure that your documents are always word perfect.

Using graphics
A picture can be worth a thousand words. Using colour, ClipArt, photos and other graphic features, make your documents even more inviting to read.

Special functions
Welcome to the Word masterclass! Here you can find out how to do some of the more challenging tasks, such as creating mail merges or newsletters. These fun and useful functions are simpler than you might expect.

WHICH VERSION OF WORD?
The information in this book is based on a PC using Microsoft Office Word 2007. If you have an earlier version of Word, you'll find that it looks different, but the functions explained in these pages are very similar or even identical.

Close up
These project-related tips offer you extra detail on various Word functions.

Key word
You'll find handy definitions of technical words or phrases here.

Bright idea
Wondering how to use your new-found skills? Look out for these tips.

GETTING AROUND THE PAGE

You're guided through every task in this book by means of illustrated steps and a range of visual features. Here are the key elements to look for on each page.

See also
Want to find out more? This panel points you towards other relevant projects for you to try.

Step-by-step
Projects are set out in clear steps. You are instructed on the keyboard and mouse commands to give, and which files and menus to access.

Useful tips
Near the main block of text are explanations of the more complex aspects of a task and alternative ways to do things.

Before you start
Projects begin with a small section of text to read. This outlines points to consider and anything you need to do before you begin.

Snapshots
Pictures of the PC screen – 'snapshots' – show you what you'll see on your own screen at each stage of the project.

Annotations
Sometimes a specific part of a step-by-step will be focused on and explained in greater depth.

Magnifications
Snapshots of the PC screen that require special attention are magnified so that you can see them more clearly.

Type in quotes
Words inside quotation marks are either the exact words you will see on screen, or what you need to type in yourself as part of a step.

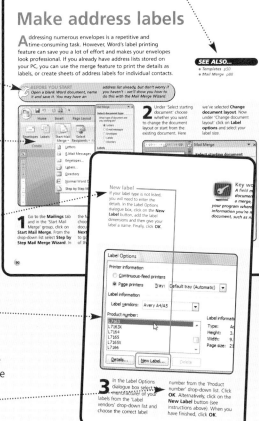

Bold type
Any bold text is a command for you to carry out. You might need to select a menu option, a toolbar button, a dialogue box tab or press a key.

Page turns
The yellow arrow indicates that your project continues over the page. The features in this book range from two pages to six.

Watch out
These tips will warn you of things to look out for that can cause a project to go wrong, and give advice on how to avoid them.

Expert advice
Advanced tips and guidance to enable you to get professional looking results from all of Word's facilities.

That's amazing!
Inspiring ideas and explanations, such as time-saving shortcuts, which you will find both interesting and useful.

Set up your PC safely

When you are choosing where you want to put your PC, check that there is adequate space and several mains sockets for all the equipment. You need to consider lighting and seating, and the amount of desk space available. If you want to send faxes from your computer or connect to the Internet, you will also need to be near a telephone wall socket.

SITTING AT YOUR COMPUTER

You need to think carefully about how to arrange your area, as a poorly laid out computer desk and PC will be irritating and may prevent you from using your computer properly.

If you find yourself leaning towards the monitor, increase the scale at which you are viewing your document.

Your legs should remain uncrossed and your knees should be lower than your hips.

An adjustable chair will support your back and can be altered to suit each family user.

Your feet should rest flat on the floor.

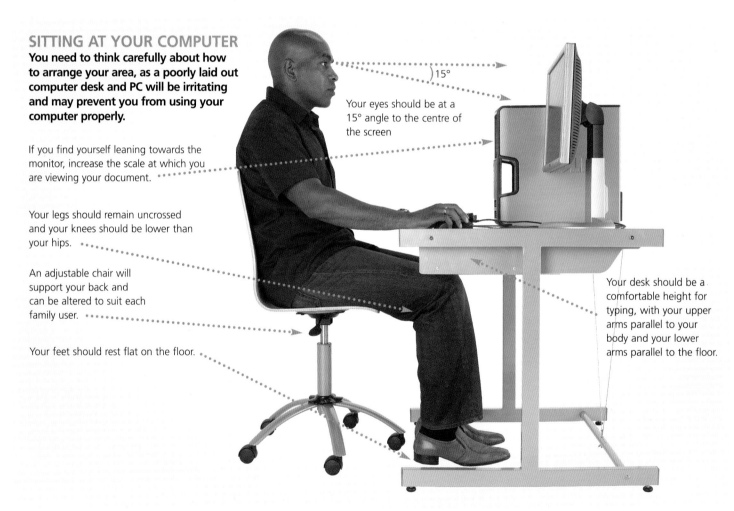

15°

Your eyes should be at a 15° angle to the centre of the screen

Your desk should be a comfortable height for typing, with your upper arms parallel to your body and your lower arms parallel to the floor.

NAMING AND PLACING PARTS

Your PC's hardware includes all the parts that you can actually see and handle. Knowing how to position these elements ensures a safe and efficient work area.

System unit

This is the part of your computer to which everything is connected. Leave space so that you can plug in the cables easily and to allow for ventilation. Don't leave cables trailing.

Printer

Position your printer near the system unit. Make sure there is sufficient space around it for loading the paper trays.

Monitor

This is the computer's screen. Position your monitor to avoid reflections, but do not face a bright window yourself as this may lead to eyestrain.

Keyboard

Make sure the keyboard is on a stable and level surface within easy reach. Leave enough space in front of it for hands and wrists. Ensure that the desk is at the correct height.

Speakers

For the best sound quality, speakers should be placed on either side of the monitor and at desk level or higher, not just pushed under the desk.

Mouse

Place the mouse to the side of your keyboard that suits whether you are left or right-handed. Use a mouse mat to create the correct amount of friction, and be sure there is plenty of room to move the mouse around.

Expert advice

If you are planning to use your computer a lot, either surfing the Internet or doing your accounts and letters, then you should invest in a good quality, comfortable office chair. Most dining chairs do not offer the support for your back that is so important when you are sitting still for long periods. Also, most office chairs are adjustable, so it will suit every member of the family. Remember, even with a comfortable chair, you should take regular 10 minute breaks to walk around.

What is Word?

Word processors are programs that enable you to create, save and print documents. Once you have created a document, you can re-use it as often as you like, making any changes and corrections you wish. Word is one of the most versatile word processors available. It makes editing and styling your documents quick, easy and fun.

SEE ALSO...

- *Explore the program* p16
- *Entering text* p20
- *Style and colour text* p30
- *Quick Access Toolbar* p68

WHAT YOU CAN DO

Word offers you an impressive range of options to help make your documents look good and save you time.

Choose from a wide range of typefaces, known as 'fonts', which you can set in different sizes, styles – such as bold, italic or underline – and colours. You can even use special effects, so the text sparkles or flashes, for example.

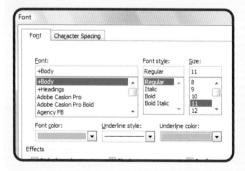

Design your page

You can set your document to the page size that suits you, choose the size of the margins, how text is aligned, and whether you want it in columns. You can insert boxes and tables, set paragraph indents, and add bullet points or automatically number lists. If you want to illustrate your text, there is a huge library of ClipArt available, or you can insert your own illustrations and photographs.

Work faster with templates

If you're not so keen on setting up documents from scratch, try using Word's ready-made templates instead. These include letterheads, memos, faxes and brochure templates.

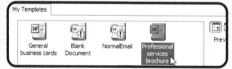

Word perfect

Word's Spelling and Grammar facility alerts you to misspelt words and badly constructed sentences. If you're stuck for an alternative word, try using the Thesaurus.

Saving time

If you need to do a mail shot, the Mail Merge facility is the perfect tool to use. Create your letter with gaps left for information, such as names and addresses. Then, using Word's step-by-step guide, merge the letter with data records that have been created in Word or ones that have been imported from a database.

Word and the Office suite

Although you can buy Word 2007 as a separate program, it usually comes as one of a suite of programs, collectively named 'Microsoft Office'. The software programs bundled in Office vary, depending on which version you buy. The version used in this publication – 'Microsoft Office Small Business Edition' – includes Excel, a spreadsheet program, PowerPoint for creating on-screen presentations with sound and animation, and Outlook, an information management program that also allows you to send and receive e-mails.

GETTING AROUND IN WORD

If this is your first time using a word processing program, you'll need a few tips to get you started.

Using the mouse

You use the mouse to point at different areas of the screen and to issue commands. It is designed to sit comfortably under your hand, with your index finger poised over the left button. You will mostly click with the left button, but sometimes you'll need to use the right. When you are following the instructions in this book, 'clicking' the mouse refers to the left button. If you need to use the right, you'll be told to 'right-click'.

When you move the mouse over text on screen, it changes from a white selection arrow to the insertion point, which looks like a capital I (see left).

If you want to enter text, click the insertion point where you want it and type. To select a button on a toolbar or a menu at the top of the screen, point the selection arrow and click.

Double-clicking the left mouse button is a speedy way to select and confirm an option.

Selecting text

To select a whole line of text, position the arrow over the white area on the left of your document,

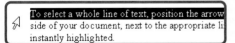

next to your chosen line, and click once. It will be highlighted instantly. To select more, or less, than one line, click in front of the first character and, with the button held down, drag the mouse over the text as far up, down, left or right as you require. Release the button when you have selected all the text you want. This is known as 'click and drag'.

To select just one word, double-click on it with your left mouse button. If you click three times, you select the whole paragraph. Once you have

selected an area of text, you can style it, change font or font size, copy and paste it into another part of the document, or delete it.

Moving around the page

You can scroll through your document by clicking on the arrows at either end of the scroll bars to the right and along the bottom of the screen, or by dragging the grey block on the scroll bar up or down.

Ribbon button commands

Near the top of the screen, below the window title, is the Ribbon. This gives you immediate access to a wide range of useful controls. Hover your mouse pointer over a button icon to display a 'pop-up' window showing the command that button performs. Some buttons, like 'Paste', for

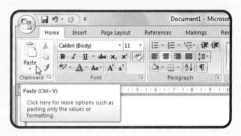

example, display a drop-down menu when you click on the button. Additionally, if applicable, the keyboard short-cut that can be used to perform the action is displayed (see list overleaf).

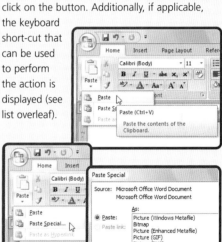

Close up
Using Word 2007, you can open a document that has been created in an older version of Word. However, you cannot use an older version of Word to open a document created in Word 2007.

USING THE KEYBOARD

Function keys are shortcuts to commands:
F1 accesses Microsoft Help and Support.
F2 is for moving text. Select your text, press **F2**, click the point on your page where you wish the text to go to and press the **Return** key.
F4 repeats your last command.

F5 opens a dialogue box for 'Find' and 'Replace' features, and 'Go To', which enables you to jump to another part of your document.
F7 checks a document for spelling and grammar.
F12 Creates a duplicate version of your document using the 'Save As' feature.

Insert allows you to type over existing text.
Delete gets rid of any selected text or item.
Home places the cursor at the start of the line.
End places the cursor at the end of the line.
Page Up places the cursor at the top of the page.
Page Down places the cursor at the page bottom.

Caps Lock causes all the letters that you type to appear as capitals.
Shift allows you to type a letter on a key as a capital or to select the topmarked option on the key. For example, pressing 'Shift' + '5' types the '%' symbol.
Ctrl and **Alt** keys, when pressed in conjunction with other keys, access different commands (keyboard shortcuts). For example, 'Ctrl' + 'P' displays the 'Print' dialogue box.
Ctrl + Alt + Delete is a useful way to quit Word, should your screen freeze up.
Windows key Accesses the Start menu.

Spacebar adds spaces between words.

Return creates a paragraph break or ends a line early. ••••••••••••••••••••

Backspace deletes text to the left of your cursor. ••••••••••••••••••••••

Arrow keys move the cursor up, down, left and right. ••••••••••••••••••••••••

Enter key works like the Return key. •••••••••••

Keyboard shortcuts

You can use all kinds of shortcuts to style your text, format your pages and access commands.

Ctrl + Shift + Spacebar creates a non-breaking space. This means that the words either side of the space are kept together on the same line.
Ctrl + Shift + hyphen creates a non-breaking hyphen. This means that a hyphenated word will not be split over two lines.
Ctrl + Q removes paragraph formatting.
Ctrl + Spacebar removes character formatting.
Ctrl + B makes text bold.
Ctrl + U underlines text.
Ctrl + I italicises text.
Ctrl + Shift + < decreases font size.
Ctrl + Shift + > increases font size.
Ctrl + F2 previews how your page will look when it is printed.
Ctrl + F4 closes the window you're working in.
Ctrl + F6 goes to the next open Word window.
Alt + F4 closes the Word program.
Alt + F8 runs a pre-recorded macro.
Alt + F10 maximises the Word window.

Close up
Use the Help menu to find out more about Word's function keys and shortcuts using Alt and Ctrl. Click the question mark icon on the right of the Ribbon and type in 'keyboard shortcuts'. Click Search.

Basics

Explore the program

Many people use Word more frequently than other programs. Although Word is designed to be intuitive, you will be able to use it more confidently and efficiently if you first take time to get to know the functions in the main document window. This will provide you with a better understanding of the many powerful features on offer.

SEE ALSO...
- *What is Word?* p12
- *Entering text* p20

BEFORE YOU START
You may have a shortcut for accessing Word on your computer Desktop. Look out for a 'Word' icon, with a small arrow in the bottom left-hand corner. Double-click on this to run Word.

1 If you don't have a Desktop shortcut to Word, click on the **Start** button, move the pointer to **All Programs** and select **Microsoft Office**. Click on **Microsoft Office Word 2007** to run the program. Once you have used Word, the program will appear as an item in your Start Menu (see above) for quick and easy access.

2 As the program opens, you will see a title window appear briefly. This tells you which version of Word you are using. After a few seconds this window disappears and the program continues to load.

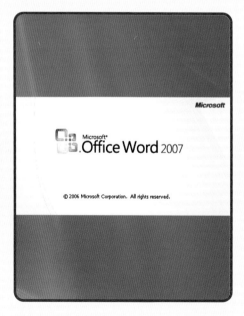

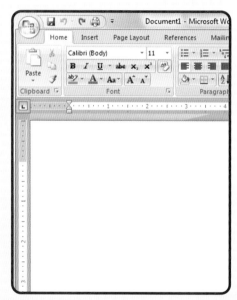

3 A blank Word document will appear on screen, into which you can start typing text. However, before you do this it is best to become acquainted with the window and the tools that you might want to use to manipulate your text.

THE DOCUMENT WINDOW

Commands for manipulating text and documents are displayed as buttons on the Ribbon and are grouped by similar functions. These are all organised within tabs. There are often different ways of accessing the same command.

Office button
Gives access to options for opening, printing and saving documents.

Command tabs
Click on a tab to access a range of related commands.

Group
Similar functions are organised within a group.

Rulers
Shows you the width of your text area and any indents or tabs you have set. Clicking and sliding the small tabs along the ruler changes the setting. The vertical ruler shows your top and bottom print margins.

Status bar
Shows the current status of your document. It tells you which page you are viewing and how many pages your document contains. It displays the number of words in the document, the spell check status and in what language dictionary was used.

Taskbar
Contains the Start button and many useful shortcuts to your programs and settings.

Quick Access Toolbar
These buttons activate common commands such as Save and Print.

Minimize button
Click here to reduce your document to a named button on the Taskbar at the bottom of the screen (see 'Minimized' button below).

Maximize/Restore button
This button enlarges the window, so it fills the screen. After maximising, the button looks like two overlapping boxes. Click again to restore the window to its previous size.

Close button
The red button with a white cross closes the program.

Cursor
The flashing cursor, or 'insertion point', appears at the start of a new document to show you where text will be inserted

Scroll bars
Use the up and down arrows to scroll up and down your document. You can also click and drag the grey block up or down to move quickly through multiple-page documents

Double arrows buttons
Click here to view the previous page (up arrows) or the following page (down arrows)

'Minimized' button
Shows which other programs/documents are currently open. Here, 'Corel Paint Shop Pro' has been minimised. Click on the button to restore the program or document.

View buttons
Click on these to change the way your document is displayed, such as a print preview or Web layout format.

Zoom level
Click and drag the slider to increase or decrease the viewing level.

COMMAND TABS

All the tasks you could want to perform in Word are displayed within groups. These are all found on the Ribbon within the different tabs.

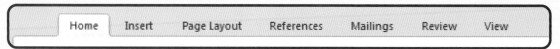

Before you start using Word, it's a good idea to click on each tab to familiarise yourself with the options it displays. Most commands have icons illustrating their function.

The Home tab
This gives you access to basic text editing and formatting functions, such as copying and pasting items and changing fonts.

The Insert tab
This allows you to add extra pages to your document and insert tables, illustrations and symbols.

The Page Layout tab
This gives you options for laying out your documents.

The References tab
Here you can access special features to enhance your documents, such as footnotes, a table of contents, cross-references, a bibliography, captions, and an index.

Expert advice
If you aren't sure what all the icons on your PC mean, go to the **Office** button and select **Word Options** then **Popular**. In the 'Top options for working with Word' section, click on the drop-down arrow next to 'ScreenTip style' and select **Show feature descriptions in ScreenTips**. Now, whenever you hover the mouse pointer over an icon the ScreenTip will tell you what it does and what the keyboard shortcut is, if there is one.

Close up
Click on the arrow, known as a dialogue box launcher, at the bottom right of a 'group' to view a dialogue box of commands for that group.

The Mailings tab

This gives you access to all the Mail Merge functions (see page 88).

The Review tab

This lets you add comments to documents and track changes made by others to your documents.

The View tab

Here you can choose how documents are displayed and whether elements such as the ruler and gridlines are shown or hidden.

CONTEXTUAL TABS

The tabs displayed on the Ribbon change depending on the action you are performing. For example, when you are editing a table the 'Table Tools' tab is displayed and when a graphic image is selected the 'Drawing Tools' tab appears, displaying additional commands to assist you.

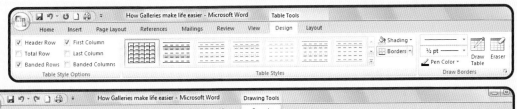

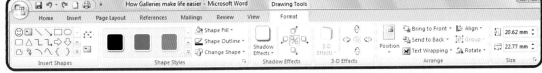

The Mini toolbar

Whenever you have text selected the Mini Toolbar will appear close by. It gives immediate access to the most commonly used text formatting options.

Highlight a piece of text and with the mouse pointer positioned over the highlighted area, slowly move the mouse upwards. The Mini Toolbar will gradually appear over the highlighted area. Click on one of the options to change your text.

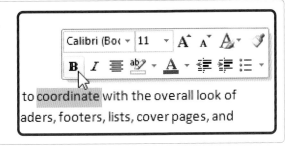

Entering text

Type in your text and you will see it appear on the page of the open document. You do not have to press the 'Return' key at the end of each line, as the text will automatically flow on to the next line. It doesn't matter if you make mistakes, as you can edit your work at any point, deleting text or moving it around the page.

SEE ALSO...
- **What is Word?** p12
- **Explore the program** p16
- **Spelling and grammar** p58

BEFORE YOU START
Open a new blank document by clicking on the **Office** button and then on **New.** In the New Document dialogue box, click on **Blank Document** and then on the **Create** button.

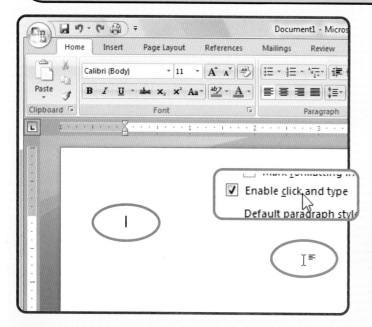

1 When you open any document the cursor appears at the start of the first page. In Print Layout view, with 'Enable click and type' ticked in 'Word Options' (see page 67), place the cursor where you want to type. The pointer shape shows the format of the text, double-click and then start typing your text.

2 In Word, text flows or 'wraps' automatically onto the next line when you reach the right-hand margin. You only need to press the Return key to start a new paragraph, or end a line early, or when making a list. Click the **Show/Hide** button in the 'Paragraph' group to reveal or hide non-printing characters, such as returns and spaces.

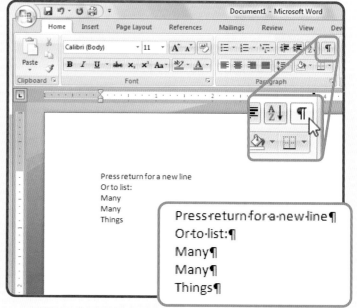

Expert advice
The keys on your computer's keyboard have different functions and different names. Some, such as the 'Shift' key, need to be held down while you press another key. Others, such as the 'Caps Lock' key, are known as toggle switches: press them once and they are switched on; press them again and they are switched off. The function keys (F1 to F12) are above the standard letter and number keys. These are used for keyboard commands.

Close up
Word can check spelling and grammar for you. A wavy red line appears under misspelt or unrecognisable words. Text that it thinks is grammatically incorrect is marked by a wavy green line.

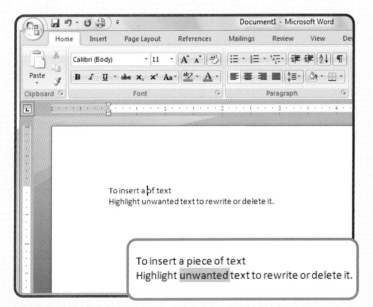

3 To insert words between existing text, move your cursor to the desired position, click and type. Use the **Backspace** key to delete errors to the left of the cursor. You can also delete text by clicking and dragging the mouse pointer over text to highlight it, then pressing the **Backspace** or the **Delete** key. Alternatively, you can highlight the text and type straight over it.

4 To type a capital letter, hold down the **Shift** key and press the letter key. Shift also causes the upper symbol on a key with two symbols, to be typed. For example, press **Shift + 5** to type '%'. If you want to type a series of capital letters, press the **Caps Lock** key. A green light on the right of your keyboard reminds you that the lock is on. To unlock it, press **Caps Lock** once more.

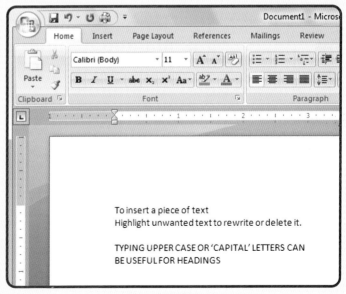

Save your work

Any new document should be saved as soon as possible after creating it, and you should continue to save any changes at regular intervals. This is important because sometimes computers crash, which means that your screen freezes and you have to exit the program without saving your files. So, if you don't save regularly, you run the risk of losing hours of work.

SEE ALSO...
● *Entering text* p20

BEFORE YOU START
To save a document for the first time, click on the **Office** button and choose **Save**.

Alternatively, you can click the **Save** *button on the Quick Access Toolbar, or use the keyboard shortcut* **Ctrl + S**.

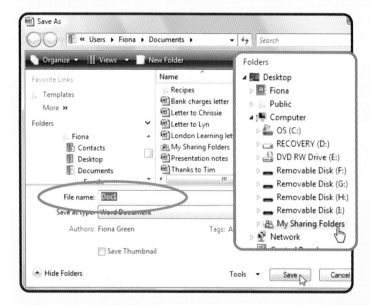

1 The first time you save a document, the Save As dialogue box opens. You will need to name your document and choose where to save it. A suggested name, usually the first line, is highlighted in the 'File name' panel. Type a name over it.
   Word prompts you to save in your 'Documents' folder. Click the arrow to the right of the panel if you want to choose a different location.

2 Your 'Documents' folder is a good place to store your work. However, it also makes sense to organise your files into subfolders – for instance, one folder for all your bank letters, another for your Web site, or a folder for each family member. If you want a new folder, click the **New Folder** icon and type in a name. To select and open the folder you wish to save into, double-click on it.

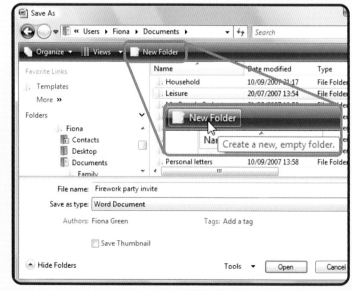

Expert advice

To save another version of a document go to the **Start** button and select **Save As.** You can then give the version a new name or choose to store it in an alternative location. This offers a quick and easy method for creating a backup file in another folder or on another disk, or for saving different versions of a file.

Bright idea

Create a template so you don't have to restyle your letters each time. Set up a page the way you want and save it. In the 'Save as type' panel, select Word Template*. **Next time you create a new document, you can choose your template from the New dialogue box.***

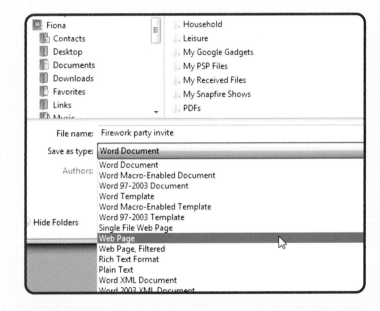

4 When you are happy with your options, click on the **Save** button. The file name in the pale grey Title bar at the top of the window changes from 'Document1', for example, to the name you have given it. As you work, you need to keep saving your changes. The quickest way is to click the 'Save' icon on the Quick Access Toolbar, top left, or press **Ctrl + S.**

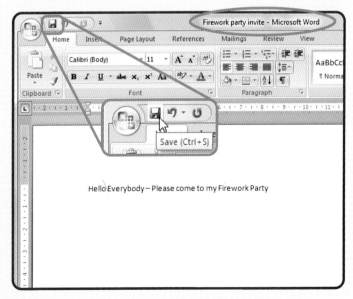

3 Choose how to save your file in the 'Save as type' panel. Most of the time you will save as a 'Word Document'. If you're creating a Web site, save your file as a 'Web Page'. 'Rich Text Format' retains your document setup, but can be opened by many other programs. 'Plain Text' saves files as text with no styling or formatting, but the text can then be read in almost any program.

Print your work

You are now ready to print out your pages. For the best results, take time to consider the appropriate layout for your document and to view how it will look before printing. Most printers allow you to vary the size of paper you use and to print envelopes and sticky labels. Depending on your printer, you may even be able to produce high quality photographic prints.

SEE ALSO...
- *Format a document* p34
- *Headers and footers* p52
- *Address labels* p90

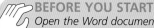

BEFORE YOU START
Open the Word document you want to print. Click on the Page Layout tab and in the 'Page Setup' group click on Margins, then Custom Margins. 'Preview' shows how the page will look.

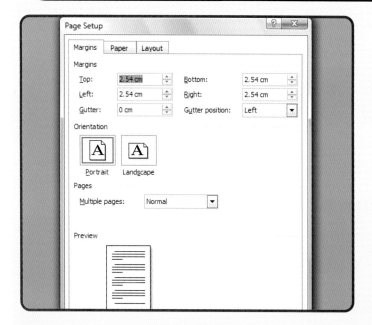

1 The margins are set to default values. To select a new value, click the up or down arrows beside each panel, or highlight the existing value and type a new number. Under 'Orientation', select **Portrait** (vertical) or **Landscape** (horizontal). See the difference between these two options in the 'Preview' section (below).

2 Select the **Paper** tab, and check that the paper size is set to 'A4'. If it isn't, or you want a different paper size, click the down arrow and select the correct paper size.

If you want to print the first page of your document on pre-printed paper (like a letterhead), you can choose the correct printer tray for that particular paper in the Paper source panel.

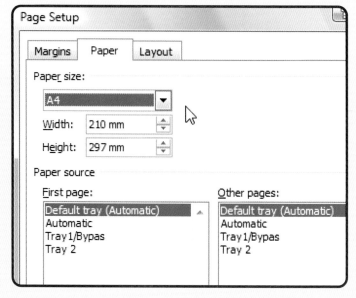

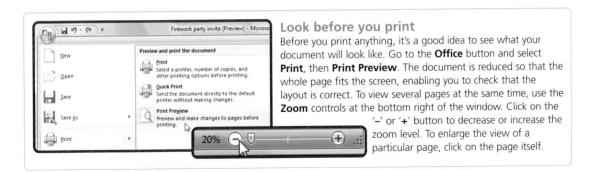

Look before you print

Before you print anything, it's a good idea to see what your document will look like. Go to the **Office** button and select **Print**, then **Print Preview**. The document is reduced so that the whole page fits the screen, enabling you to check that the layout is correct. To view several pages at the same time, use the **Zoom** controls at the bottom right of the window. Click on the '–' or '+' button to decrease or increase the zoom level. To enlarge the view of a particular page, click on the page itself.

4 Go to the **Office** button and click **Print**. Select your printer in the 'Name' panel. Under 'Page range', you can choose to print the whole document ('All'), the page you are on ('Current page'), or a range of pages ('Pages'). To print a range, you will need to enter the page numbers. You can print an area of text that you have highlighted by using the 'Selection' button.

3 Finally, click the **Layout** tab to change the position of the headers and footers in the 'From edge' section. Under 'Page' in the 'Vertical alignment' box, you can choose how your text is positioned between the top and bottom page margins. Text is automatically aligned to the top. You can number your lines and create borders for sections of text or whole pages. Click **OK** to finish.

Bright idea
Printer ink cartridges are expensive. Printing documents out in black and white is a much cheaper option than using colour print, so save the colour for essential jobs.

Expert advice
You can stop printing, even after you've given the Print command. When you click **OK** in the Print dialogue box, a progress window appears on screen, containing 'Stop', 'Pause' and 'Reprint' buttons. If this box is not showing, click on the **Printer** icon on the Taskbar at the bottom of your screen to see it.

6 For double-sided printing, scroll down the options in the 'Print' box and select **Odd pages**. Pages 1, 3, 5 and so on will then print. Once these are done, turn the printed sheets over, place them in your printer again and select **Even pages** in the Print dialogue box. Click **OK** to print pages 2, 4, 6 and so on.

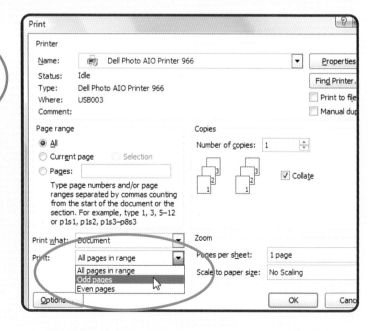

5 To print more than one copy of a document, click on the up arrow in the 'Number of copies' panel, or highlight the figure and type in the number of copies you want. Select the **Collate** option if you want your copies printed in page order within each set.

Styling Your Text

Choose and size a font

The appearance of any document can be changed dramatically through the use of different fonts, or 'typefaces', and by making text such as headings a different size. With Word, you even have the ability to use many different fonts and sizes on any page to create exactly the overall effect that you are looking for.

SEE ALSO...
- *Style and colour text p30*
- *Format a document p34*

BEFORE YOU START
To change text to a different font, highlight the text that you want to change. You can then choose to make individual changes quickly, or to make several changes at once.

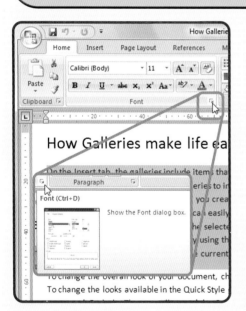

1 When you want to make several changes to your text – to alter font, size and style all at once, for example – it is quicker to do everything at the same time using the Font dialogue box. Click on the **Font** dialogue box launcher to open the dialogue box.

2 The default font for the template you are using is highlighted in the 'Font' panel. A line of your own text is shown in this default font in the 'Preview' pane at the bottom.
To view the text in a different font, scroll down the list in the 'Font' panel. Select a font name and look again in the 'Preview' pane to see your text displayed in the selected font.

3 Scroll through, select and view different typefaces (some of them have symbols, not letters). When you have chosen, click **OK** to confirm it. To change the default font for a template you are using, select a font and click on the **Default** button, then on **OK**. This changes the document and the template.

Serif or sans-serif

Two common fonts in use today are 'Times New Roman' and 'Arial'. 'Times New Roman' was developed as a typeface for *The Times* newspaper and is a serif font. This means that there are short, fine lines at the ends of the strokes of each character – this was thought to lead the eye smoothly from one letter to the next. 'Arial' was developed later, and is a sans-serif (without serif) font. Research has shown that a serif font is generally more readable when used in long documents, but that a sans-serif font is clearer for anyone who is partially sighted.

Times New Roman
Arial

Key word
The height of a font is measured in points, and there are precisely 72 points to an inch (2.5cm). A standard 12-point font measures one-sixth of an inch (4mm) in height on the page.

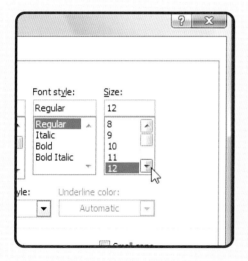

4 Using the arrows, scroll and select a font size from the list. If the size you want is not there, click on the box and type a figure, then press **Return** and your text will change.

The largest standard font size is 72 point. If you need a bigger size, try using WordArt (see page 84). There are also various text effects to choose from, including shadows and embossed type.

5 You can make individual changes to text more quickly by using the formatting buttons on the Ribbon. To alter the font, highlight your text and click on the down arrow to the right of the 'Font' panel. A drop-down list gives all the fonts available, with their names displayed in the associated typeface.

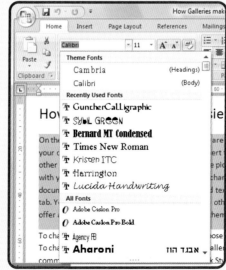

6 For quick changes to the size of an item of text, highlight it, then click on the down arrow to the right of the 'Font Size' box found in the 'Font' group. A drop-down menu lists point sizes. Click on one to select it.

29

Style and colour text

Changing the style of your text is a sure way to alter the look of a document and draw the reader's attention to specific points that you wish to make. You can add emphasis and different styles to your characters by using some of the specific enhancements, such as italics, or by underlining and colouring parts of your text.

SEE ALSO...
- *Choose and size a font p28*
- *Format a paragraph p36*

BEFORE YOU START
*Highlight the text you want to make changes to, and click on the **Font** dialogue box launcher in the 'Font' group. Use this box to make several different changes to a piece of text.*

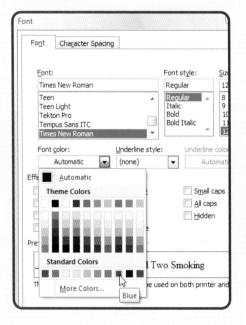

1 Select the style you wish to use in the 'Font style' panel. For emphasis, choose to embolden (Bold) or italicise (Italic) headings, rather than underlining them. Italicised text can look smaller than regular text, so you might want to embolden it, too. View changes in the 'Preview' pane.

2 To alter the colour of your selected text, click on the arrow by the 'Font color' panel. Select a colour by clicking on one of the square colour buttons. In the 'Preview' pane, you will see your coloured text.

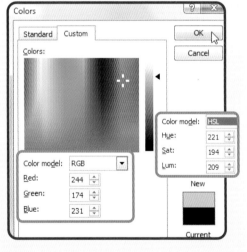

3 For a wider range of colours, click on **More Colors**. Select the **Standard** tab or the **Custom** tab for further choices. Click on a colour and it appears in the smaller 'New' pane.

Under the 'Custom' tab, you can customise the colour via the 'Color model' options for RGB (Red, Green, Blue) and HSL (Hue, Saturation, Luminescence). Click **OK** to finish.

Bright idea
'Hidden' text, which is one of the 'Effects' options, allows you to make notes in your document which will show on the computer screen but will not print out.

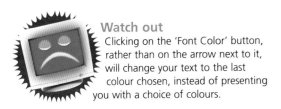

5 Click on the box of your choice in the 'Effects' section to select a further style. 'Superscript' is used for above-the-line text items like dates (16th), while 'Subscript' is for below-the-line items like 'H_2O'. Visual effects such as 'Emboss' and 'Engrave' can look faint in print depending on their colour.

Strikethrough — Lock, Stock and Two Smok
Double Strikethrough — Lock, Stock and Two Smok
Superscript — Lock, Stock and Two Smokin
Subscript — Lock, Stock and Two Smokin
Shadow — Lock, Stock and Two Smok
Outline — Lock, Stock and Two Smok
Emboss — Lock, Stock and Two Smok
Engrave — Lock, Stock and Two Smok
Small Caps — LOCK, STOCK AND TWO SM
All Caps — LOCK, STOCK AND TWO
Hidden

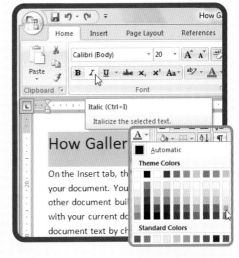

4 Click on the arrow beside 'Underline style' for a drop-down list of line styles. Use the scroll bar to move up and down. Click on a style to select it, then click on the arrow beside 'Underline color' to select a colour for the line.

6 If you want to use only one of these functions, it is quicker to use the button icons in the 'Font' group. You can change the font colour, as well as embolden, italicise and underline selected text. However, these buttons have limited functions. For example, you cannot underline in colour, nor can you access all the 'Effects' in the Font dialogue box.

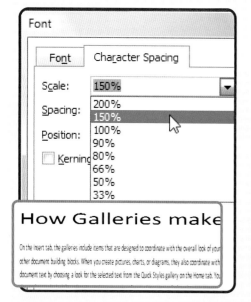

7 In the Font dialogue box, click on the **Character Spacing** tab. If you have different font sizes within your selected text, and you want to scale the size of the text up or down without altering the font sizes, select a percentage from the 'Scale' box.

8 Imagine you have typed a heading, or your address, at the top of a page or column. You have centred the text, but the letters look too tightly squeezed together – you want to stretch them across without altering the font size. Click on the down arrow in the 'Spacing' box and select **Expanded** and use the 'By' box to define an amount. Select **Condensed** to do the opposite.

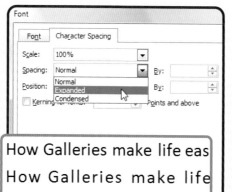

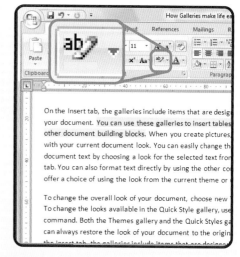

9 If you need to, you can emphasise a portion of your text to make it appear as if it has been marked by a highlighter pen. First, using your mouse, click and drag through the relevant text. Then in the 'Font' group click on the text highlighter button. If you want to highlight text in a different colour, click on the arrow to the right of the button, and make your selection.

Styling Your Document

Format a document

The overall appearance of a document is determined by the formatting characteristics set up within the template in which you open it. You may want to add a new heading or items such as page numbers. If a pre-set heading is not quite perfect, you can modify it. If you work on many documents of the same type, you may even want to create your own style and save it as a template.

SEE ALSO...
- *Choose a font* p28
- *Format a paragraph* p36
- *AutoFormat* p46

BEFORE YOU START
Templates for document formats are sub-divided into various styled paragraph and character items. If you are happy with the style options in the template, use AutoFormat (see p46).

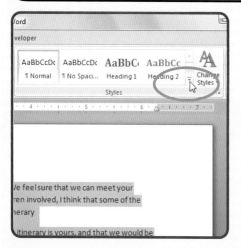

1 Highlight your text. With the 'Home' tab selected, click on the down-pointing arrow in the 'Styles' group. A drop-down list displays styles available for the current document.

Hover you mouse pointer over any of the pre-set paragraph styles and your highlighted text will be displayed in that style. Move your mouse pointer away to revert to the original style. Click on a particular style to select it permanently.

2 Alternatively, click on the dialogue box launcher on the right of the 'Styles' group to view the 'Styles' pane, which lists additional pre-set styles. Hover the pointer over a style to check its details – if you want to use it click on its name to select it.

Click on the arrow on the right of the 'Show' panel for formatting and style options. For example, choose 'All styles' to view the available formatting styles.

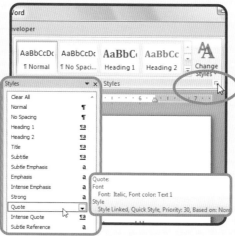

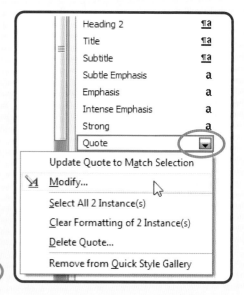

3 Styles are defined as either paragraph ('¶'), character(s) ('a') or both ('¶a'), to show whether they apply to a paragraph or words.

To alter a style, select it in the 'Styles' pane and when the icon to its right changes to a down arrow, click on it to reveal a list of options. Click on **Modify**.

Themes

You can style text using 'themes' which will give an integrated look to your document, ensuring that fonts, colours and related graphics, such as 'bullets', all work well together. To utilise this option, click on the **Page Layout** tab and select **Themes**. Browse through the themes in the gallery and hover your mouse pointer over an item to view your document in that theme.

Watch out

If you save changes to the original template, you can end up with a whole mixture of muddled styles. It is better to save new or modified styles as a new template, giving it a name you will recognise. To do this, click on the **Office** button, then **Save As** and select **Word Template** in the 'Save as type' panel.

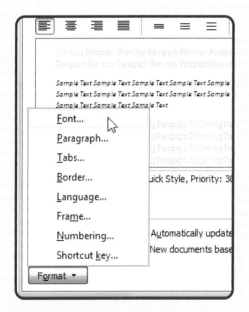

4 Click on the **Format** button to access a drop-down menu. Select and change any style details by clicking on each heading to open the appropriate dialogue box.

You can change the font and size, paragraphing, indents and so on.

5 Select 'New documents based on this template' only if you wish to use the modified style in new documents based on this template. Select 'Automatically update' to update all previous instances of that style in your document. Click on **OK** to modify the formatting for the selected paragraph and to return to the document.

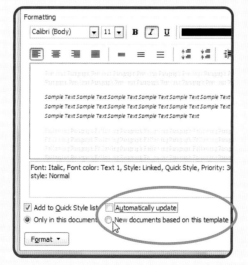

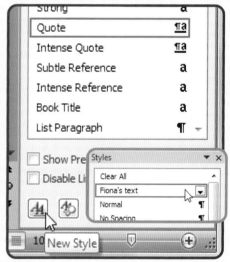

6 Click on the **New Style** button at the bottom of the 'Styles' pane to create a new style. Name it and modify items, selecting and defining those you need. You can add to the list at any time. Use the new styles in your document and save a version of the document as a template which you can use for similar documents.

Format a paragraph

Just as you can easily change the look of your entire document, so you can also change the layout, or 'format', of individual sections within it. Quoted text can be indented, either from the left or from both sides, while hanging indents can give a traditional look to your work. You can also prevent a single line straying on to the next page, or being left behind.

SEE ALSO...
● *Format a document* *p34*
● *Using tabs* *p40*
● *AutoFormat* *p46*

BEFORE YOU START
*Highlight several paragraphs or click anywhere in a single paragraph to select it. Click on the dialogue box launcher in the 'Paragraph' group, then on the **Indents and Spacing** tab.*

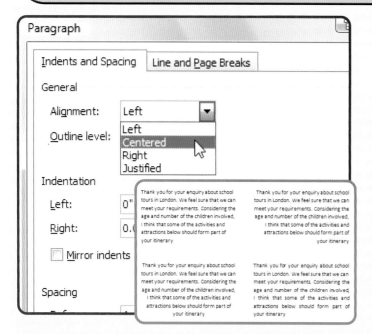

1 In the 'Alignment' panel, **Left** is already selected by default, so your text is lined up to the left side of the page. Click on the arrow to the right to select 'Centered' (text is centred on the page), 'Right' (to make it line up to the right side of the page), or 'Justified' (to stretch and align the text so that it is straight on both sides).

2 Under 'Indentation', select the 'Left' or 'Right' panel and scroll down to set how far in from the left or right edge of the page to place the text. This is good for indenting quotes.

Click in the 'Special' panel and select **First line**. Click **By** to determine how far in from the main body of the paragraph the first line will be set. Select **Hanging** to indent all lines in a paragraph except for the first.

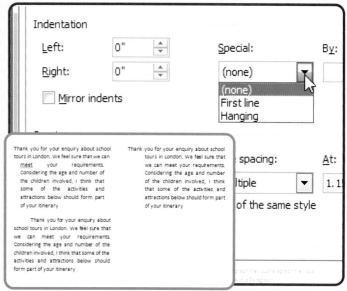

Ribbon shortcuts

You can also set the alignment by clicking on the alignment buttons in the 'Paragraph' group.

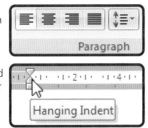

Paragraph indents can be changed by using the small 'Indent' markers at either end of the ruler at the top of the screen. Let your mouse hover over them. 'ScreenTips' show four types on the left: 'First Line', 'Left Margin', 'Hanging Indent', and 'Left Indent'.

Hanging Indent

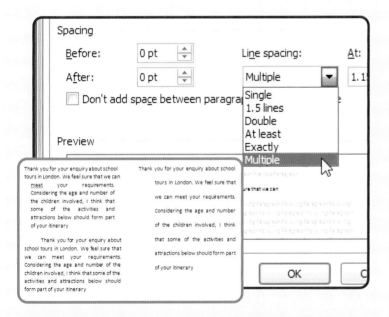

3 Select the 'Before' and 'After' panels to specify how much space will run before and after paragraphs in the selected text. Click in the 'Line spacing' panel to alter the spacing between lines within the paragraph. Letters are usually 'single' spaced, while typing draft documents in 'double spacing' leaves room for corrections. You can also set an exact amount of space or multiple lines.

4 Click on the **Line and Page Breaks** tab. The 'Widow/Orphan control' option stops the last line of a paragraph appearing by itself at the top of the following page, or the first line being left on its own at the bottom of the previous page. You can also fine-tune paragraph breaks and opt to remove line numbers, or to turn off automatic hyphenation of words in this tab.

Using columns and bullets

One very effective way of changing the appearance of your document is to put your text in columns. Try this with documents such as newsletters as it makes large amounts of text much easier to read. Alternatively, adding bullet points will help to display lists in a more accessible and logical way, while improving the overall look of your document.

SEE ALSO...
- *Format a document* p34
- *Using tabs* p40
- *Using tables* p48

BEFORE YOU START
Although you can format text into columns after you have finished typing, it is sensible to set the number of columns first, so you have a rough idea of how your pages will look.

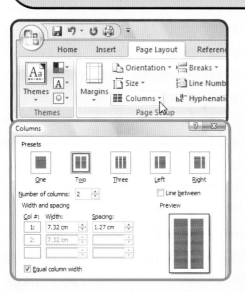

1 In the 'Page Layout' tab, click on **Columns** in the 'Page Setup' group, then on **More Columns**. In the dialogue box, select the number of columns, either by choosing one of the presets or by typing the number into the panel. Then, either tick 'Equal column width' for evenly spaced columns, or specify each column width individually.

2 Your column format will apply to the whole of the document, unless you specify otherwise. If, for example, you need a heading, enter this first, leave a few line spaces and then set up your column format. In the dialogue box, make sure you have selected **This point forward** in the 'Apply to' panel.
The 'line between' option allows you to put a visible line between your columns. Click **OK** when your formatting is complete.

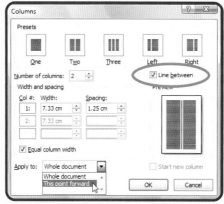

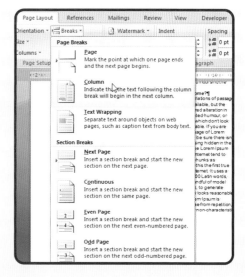

3 The cursor appears in your first column for you to begin typing. When the first column is full, your text will run straight into the next one. To force text over into the next column, position your cursor where you want the break, click on the **Page Layout** tab, select **Breaks** from the 'Page Setup' group and then click on **Column**.

Use your ruler

Column width can be altered quickly using the ruler at the top of the page. Blue areas relate to margins between the columns. Click the edge of a column and drag it to the required size. If you select equal column width, all columns will alter to match. You can change page margins in the same way.

Numbered lists

These can be created, customised and new styles defined, using the processes explained in steps 1 and 2 below. To start using the 'Numbering' features click on the down arrow to the right of the 'Numbering' icon in the 'Paragraph' group.

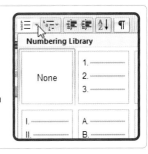

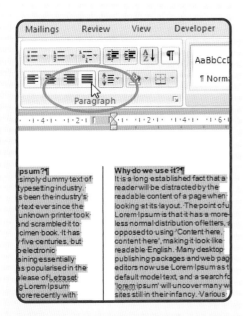

1 To give your text added emphasis, use bullet points. Click on the down arrow to the right of the 'bullet' icon in the 'Paragraph' group. The dialogue box that appears gives you a range of bullet point styles to choose from. Click to select a style of bullet in the 'Bullet Library', then click **OK**. Each time you press **Return** in your text, a new bullet will be added.

2 To create your own bulleted style, click on **Define New Bullet**, at the bottom of the 'Bullet Library'. In the dialogue box click on the **Symbol** button to display characters from the 'Symbol' font. Select a character, then click **OK**. Choose an option from the 'Alignment' panel, and check your selections in the 'Preview' pane. When finished, click **OK**. Your new bullet style now appears in the library.

4 Your text can then be styled and formatted in the normal way. To avoid awkward line ends in narrow columns, it is a good idea to justify your text. This will give it a more professional look. Highlight the text and click on the **Justify** icon in the 'Paragraph' group.

Using tabs

The 'Tab' feature allows you to align your text – or 'tabulate' it. This is a quick way of moving words across the page, rather than pressing the spacebar repeatedly. While you would create a table to organise lots of information into columns and rows, tabs are a handy way of tidying up a letter, an invoice, or a few simple columns of information.

SEE ALSO...

● *Using columns and bullets* p38
● *Using tables* p48
● *Sort a list* p96

BEFORE YOU START
When you are working with tabs, it is a good idea to have the tabs showing.

Click on the Show/Hide button in the 'Paragraph' group to reveal them, if they are not already visible.

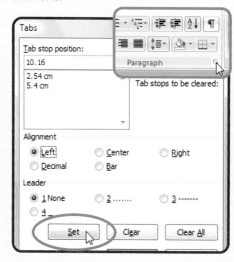

1 Microsoft Word opens with tabs set at the default position of 0.5 inches or metric equivalent. Pressing the **Tab** key on your keyboard causes the cursor to jump along the line to these preset positions.

2 To set your own tabs instead of using the defaults, highlight the document or the section to which tabs should apply. Click on the dialogue box launcher in the 'Paragraph' group and, with the 'Indents and Spacing' tab selected, click on **Tabs**. Enter the position of your first tab in the 'Tab stop position' panel. Add more tabs, clicking **Set** after each one.

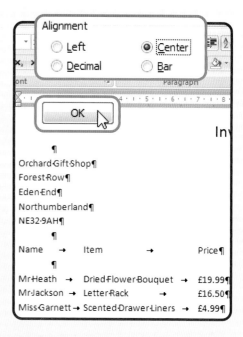

3 The Tabs dialogue box also allows you to change the alignment of your tabs. The default setting is aligned to the left, but you can align the tabs to the middle ('Center') of the text or to the right.

Tab shortcut

A quick way to set your tabs is by using the ruler at the top of the page. Highlight your text. Then, simply by clicking on the ruler at the required tab position, a left-aligned tab will be set. To change the alignment, click on the top left-hand corner to change the icon from left to centre or right-aligned tabs.

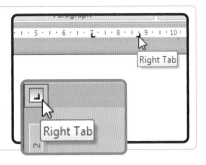

Bright idea
If you prefer to work in inches go to the Tools *menu and select* Options. *Select the* General *tab and look under 'Measurement units' for a drop-down list that offers you a choice of units. Select* Inches *then click* OK.

5 A further option allows you to fill in the space between your tabs with a type of line called a leader. The default setting is 'none', but you can select from the options beneath 'Leader' to insert dots, a broken line or a solid line. These options work especially well when you are displaying columns of figures.

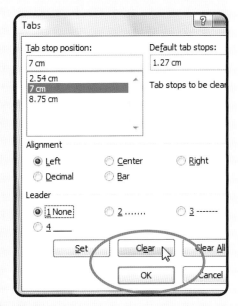

4 If your tabulated text includes figures, select the Decimal alignment button. This aligns all your numbers at the decimal point. Selecting Bar gives you a vertical dividing line at the position of the tab.

6 The bottom of the Tabs dialogue box has a number of buttons. To delete a tab you've set, select it and click **Clear**. Click **Clear All** to automatically remove all of your tabs.
   When you're happy with your settings, click **OK** to return to your document.

Design a letterhead

Using a personalised letterhead will add a touch of flair and individuality to all your correspondence. Once you've created one letterhead, you can follow the same principles to design letterheads for different circumstances – one for business stationery, perhaps. Save your letterhead as a template and you can use it whenever you write a letter.

SEE ALSO...
- Choose a font *p28*
- Format a document *p34*
- Headers and footers *p52*

BEFORE YOU START
*Create a new document by clicking on the **Page Layout** tab and then on the **Page Setup** dialogue box launcher. Click on the **Layout** tab, set up the margins and the Header size. Click **OK**.*

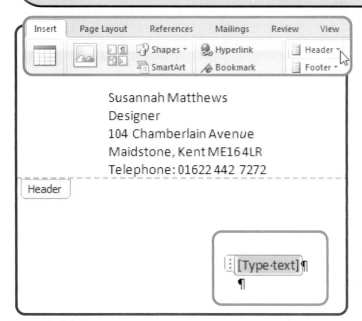

1 A good way to create your letterhead is within the 'Header' section of your document. Go to the **Insert** tab and from the 'Header and Footer' group, click on **Header** and then select **Blank** from the drop-down list of styles. Type your name, address and other contact details in the **[Type text]** prompt area.

2 Highlight your name, click on the **Home** tab, then on the **Font** dialogue box launcher and select a font, style and size, hovering the mouse pointer over these to view them in the Preview window. Then click on **OK**. Style your address in the same manner.

Key word
The terms header and footer describe the information that appears at the top (header) and bottom (footer) of each page of a document – for example, running titles, reference details and page numbers.

Bright idea
If you have an e-mail address or Web site, remember to include them in your letterhead.

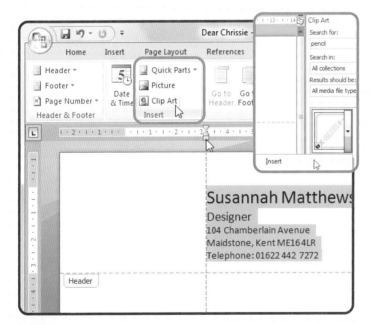

3 You can also add a Clip Art image to your letterhead. To make space, highlight your text, then click and drag the left indent marker on the ruler. Go to the 'Insert' group and click on **Clip Art**. Type a keyword in the 'Search for' panel in the clip art pane and click on **Go**. Click on an image and select **Insert** in the pop-up menu.

4 Go to the 'Arrange' group and click on **Text Wrapping**, then select **Square**. Click on the image and then drag it to reposition it on the left of the text. You can resize the image by clicking and dragging on one of the corner handles. Then click on **Close Header and Footer** on the far right of the Ribbon.

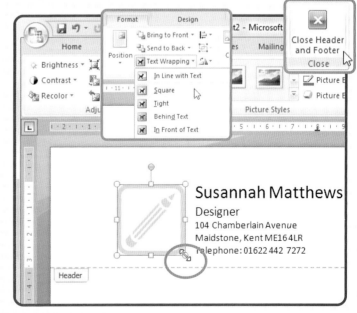

Use your toolbar
The toolbar buttons at the top of the screen help you to style your text quickly. Highlight the text. Click on the relevant button to make it bold, to italicise it or to underline it. Change the position of your text, too, by clicking on the 'Left', 'Center', 'Right' or 'Justify' alignment buttons.

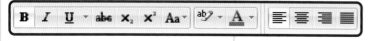

Bright idea
Save time and effort by using Word's automatic dating facility for letters. Click where you want the date to appear in your document, go to the Insert *tab and select* Date and Time. *In the dialogue box choose your preferred style and click* OK.

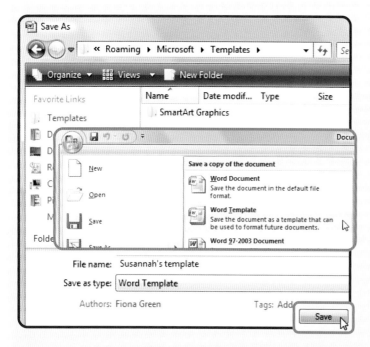

5 When you are happy with your design, save it as a template so that you can use it repeatedly. Click on the **Microsoft Office** button and select **Save As**, then **Word Template**. Give the template a name, select a suitable folder to save it in, and click on **Save**.

6 To use your template, click on the **Microsoft Office** button and select **New**. Under Templates in the left pane click on **My Templates**. In the New dialogue box that appears, select your new template and then click on **OK** to create a new document.

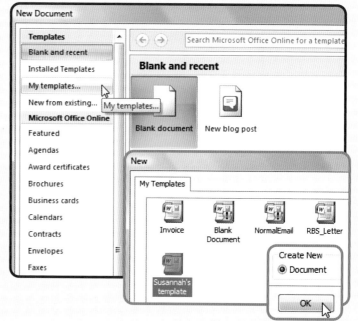

Changing your template

Start by clicking on the **Microsoft Office** button and selecting **Open**. In the Open dialogue box, under 'Favorite Links' in the left-hand pane, select **Templates**. Then, in the right-hand pane, locate the template that you want to change, click on it and then on **Open**. Make your changes and then save it. Your template is now updated and ready to use.

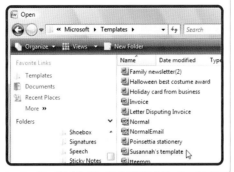

7 The cursor will flash below your letterhead. Press the **Return** key to create a few blank lines and then type your letter. To save the document, click on the **Microsoft Office** button and select **Save As**, then click on **Word Document** from the options on the right.

8 When the Save As dialogue box appears, click on **Documents**. At this point you can select a subfolder or create a new folder by clicking on the New Folder button if you wish. Type in a name for your document and click on **Save**. This letter will be saved, while your letterhead template is preserved for you to re-use.

AutoFormat your text

The AutoFormat feature applies standard headings and text styles to your documents, giving them a professional finish. You can choose exactly how to format your text and then either have your work formatted automatically as you type, or format a whole document when you have completed it. Word enables you to review and accept or reject the changes.

SEE ALSO...
- *Format a document* *p34*
- *Templates* *p50*
- *AutoCorrect your text* *p62*

CHOOSE YOUR STYLE

Whether you are typing a letter or an e-mail, Word can style your page to suit your needs.

Formatting text as you type

To format your text automatically as you type, you need to tell Word what you want it to change. Go to the **Microsoft Office** button and

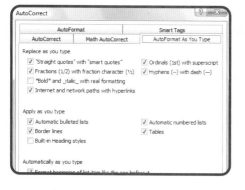

click on **Word Options**. In the Word Options dialogue box select **Proofing** in the left pane, and then click on **AutoCorrect Options** in the right pane. Click on the **AutoFormat As You Type** tab and select the options you require. If you want to wait until you have finished before using AutoFormat, untick all of these boxes.

Formatting an existing document

When you have finished typing and are ready to format your document, click on the **AutoFormat** button on the Quick Access toolbar (see below). If you want Word to do this without input from you, select 'AutoFormat now'. Otherwise, click 'AutoFormat and review each change' so

that you can approve changes. Unless instructed, Word formats text as a general document. If you want a letter or an e-mail format, click on the drop-down menu beneath 'Please select a document type...' and choose from the list.

Click on **Options** for preferred settings, which are mostly the same as those on the 'AutoFormat As You Type' tab. However, a few options at the top and bottom of the dialogue boxes differ.

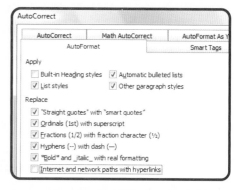

Close up
If you're AutoFormatting a list as you type it, you'll need to tell Word when you've finished the list. To do this, either press the Return key twice, or press it once and then press the Backspace key once.

Quick access to AutoFormat
To add the AutoFormat command to the Quick Access Toolbar, click on the **Microsoft Office** button, and then on **Word Options**. Click on **Customize**. In the Word Options dialogue box under 'Choose commands from', click on **All commands**. Scroll down the list and click on **Autoformat** and then click on **Add**. You can also add the **AutoFormat Now** command in the same way.

Some of your AutoFormat options

Built-in Headings Select this option when Word

formats a completed document, but leave it unticked when Word formats as you type, as it is easier to apply heading styles when you have an overview of the whole document.

List styles Tick this box if you want to apply the standard style for bulleted and numbered lists. Word removes any bullets or numbers that you've inserted and replaces them with preset styles. Select the **Styles** box in the 'Preserve' section to

retain any styles you applied to your document when you ran AutoFormat. This option is only available for completed documents. Choose your options, then click **OK** and **OK** again. After a few seconds, your page is reformatted, and the AutoFormat dialogue box appears.

Reviewing changes

If you like the way the document looks, click **Accept All**. If you don't like it, click **Reject All**.

Alternatively, you can go through the entire document, accepting and rejecting each formatting change. Click **Review Changes**. Your text reappears with blue and red 'invisibles', indicating formatting changes that have been made. An explanation of each change is given in the dialogue box.

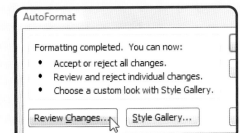

Accepting or rejecting changes

If you're happy with a formatting change, click the ➪ **Find** button to accept it and jump to the next change. If you don't like a change, click the **Reject** button to undo it. If you reject a change and then decide to keep it after all, click the **Undo** button on the Formatting toolbar.

To see what the document looks like without the distracting revision marks, select the **Hide Marks** button. When you've finished reviewing the changes, click **Cancel**. To apply the formats you've accepted, click the **Accept All** button in the AutoFormat dialogue box.

Choosing a different look

If you want to change the appearance of your document completely, go to the Quick Access toolbar and click on the **AutoFormat** button.

Make sure the 'Auto Format and review each change' option is selected and click **OK**. Now click the **Style Gallery** button (see left).

All the document templates are displayed in the left pane. Click on a template and then under 'Preview' select 'Document' to update the 'Preview of' pane on the right.

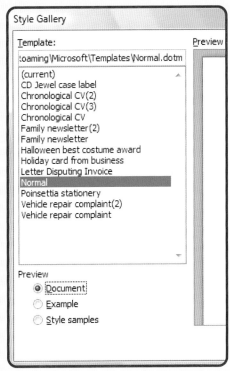

Alternatively, select **Example** in the 'Preview' section, to preview a sample document. Click **OK**, and then close the dialogue box.

Bright idea
If you are unhappy with the way that AutoFormat has changed your pages, press the Undo button on the Quick Access toolbar.

Key word
Invisibles are the symbols used to represent specific instances of formatting in a document, such as a paragraph break, indent or tab. They are only for visual reference on screen, and do not print with the rest of your document.

Using tables

Tables provide an ideal structure for organising and presenting information. Table data can be sorted alphabetically, numerically, or by date, and you can treat the table like a mini-spreadsheet and use it to perform calculations. Word 2007 also lets you move the table around the page, or position it exactly where you want within text.

SEE ALSO...
- *Using columns and bullets* p38
- *Using tabs* p40
- *Templates* p50

BEFORE YOU START
Think about how many columns and rows you are likely to need – a rough sketch might help you to decide. Extra rows are easy to add, but new columns require a little more sorting out.

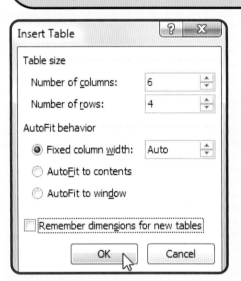

1 Click on the **Insert** tab, then on **Table**, and **Insert Table**. Select the required number of columns and rows in the dialogue box. 'Fixed column width' spreads columns evenly across the page. 'AutoFit to contents' widens columns to fit typed text or graphics, while 'AutoFit to window' allows the table to fit a Web browser window.

2 Type in your text. To move from cell to cell, press the **Tab** key, or use your mouse to position your cursor. You can type any amount of text in a cell, as the size of all the cells in that row will increase to accommodate it.

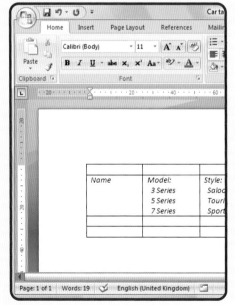

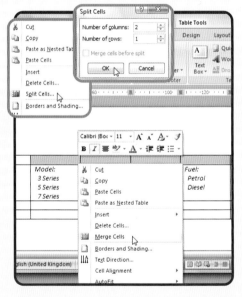

3 To merge cells together – to create a heading, for example – click and drag your mouse over the cells to select them. Right-click and select **Merge Cells**. To split cells, to create more than originally specified, highlight the cell or row, right-click and select **Split Cells**. Specify the number of columns. Click **OK**.

Formatting your table

To customise your table, highlight it, then right-click on the small '+' symbol at the top left of the table, and select **Table Properties** from the drop-down list. From here, you can alter the position of your table on the page and the way text wraps around it. Clicking on the **Borders and Shading** button allows you to alter the appearance of each cell and to show or hide as much of the grid as needed.

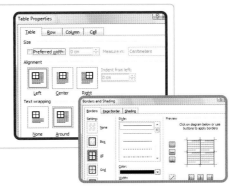

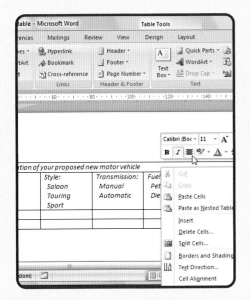

4 Having merged your cells to create a heading over the columns below, key in the text for your heading. Right-click and from the drop-down list that appears, click on the **centered alignment button**. You can style an individual cell, a complete column or row in the same manner.

5 For a more complex, customised table, click on the **Insert** tab, then on **Table** and choose **Draw Table**. Your cursor changes to a pencil shape. Click and drag diagonally, to draw the outline of your table. Then click and drag horizontally across the table to create rows, and vertically to create columns. As you drag, a dotted line indicates the position of the line.

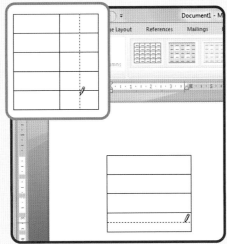

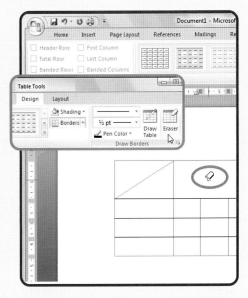

6 The 'Design' tab displays tools to help format and modify your table. Click on **Eraser**, in the 'Draw Borders' group, then on a line to remove it. Click on the **Line Style**, **Line Weight** and **Pen Colour** options in the 'Draw Borders' group to change the appearance of your table.

Templates

Every time you create a new document in Word 2007, you are offered the 'Blank Document' template, which is an empty document with a pre-defined layout. However, there are a variety of other templates available, some already installed on your system and numerous others available from the Microsoft Office Online collection.

SEE ALSO...
- *Design a letterhead* *p42*
- *Make address labels* *p90*

BEFORE YOU START
Office 2007 has a huge list of ready made templates which you can use as a base and adapt for your requirements. In this project, we are creating a formal letter.

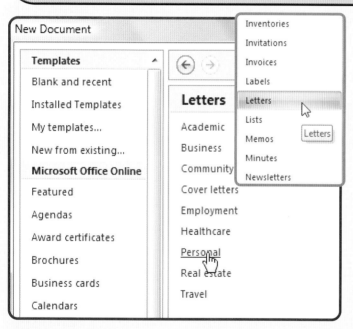

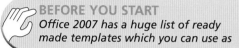

1 Click on the **Office** button, then on **New**. This opens the New Document pane. Under the 'Microsoft Office Online' section of the pane on the left, scroll down the list to find the category that you are looking for, here 'Letters'. Click on **Letters**, then from the pane on the right, click on **Personal**.

2 In the middle panel you will now see a selection of thumbnail images of different types of pre-formed letter templates. Click on an image to preview a larger version in the right panel. Select a style, in this case 'Vehicle repair complaint', and click on **Download**.

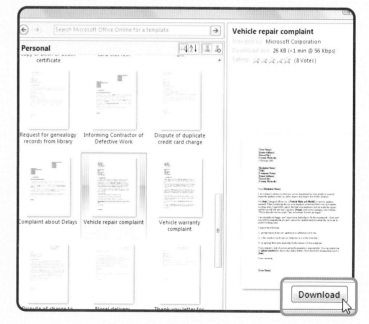

That's amazing!
You can create your own templates to re-use as often as you wish. To save a document as a template, click on the **Office** button, then **Save As**. Name your file. In the 'Save as type' panel, select **Word Template**. Your new template will be added to the templates available when you create a new document.

Watch out
Many of the templates provided by Word were created specifically for American users. This means that they may not always be appropriate in the UK.

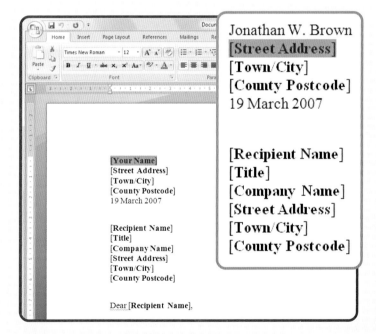

3 Your downloaded letter will have bracketed bold 'Prompt' areas within it. Click inside the brackets to highlight the prompt, and type your own details where appropriate. Other areas of the letter will need modifying, so highlight these as you go through and insert your own details. Delete any prompts that are not appropriate.

4 Now you can style and personalise your letter. For example, highlight your name and address at the top of the letter, then go to the **Home** tab and click on the **Font** dialogue box launcher. Select a font, style and size, clicking on any that interest you to view them in the Preview window. Make your selection then click **OK**.

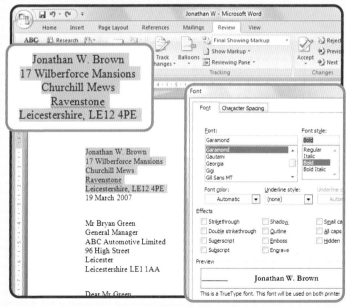

Headers and footers

Headers and footers enable you to add running information to your pages, such as page numbers. They appear in the top or bottom margins of your document, outside the normal print area. Anything that you insert in a header or footer appears on every page of your document, unless you specify otherwise.

BEFORE YOU START
*To add a header or footer to a document, click on the **Insert** tab and then on either **Header** or **Footer**, from the 'Header & Footer' group. Select a style from the drop-down list.*

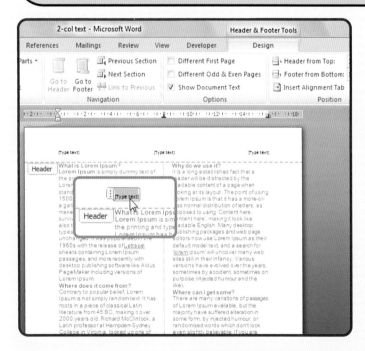

1 Here we have chosen the 'Blank (Three Columns)' style from the drop-down list. To enter the data for your 'Header' click once in the left-hand **[Type text]** prompt. When active the background will have a blue highlight (see inset).

2 Type your text inside the first prompt (left), for example, your name. Then click in the third prompt (right) and type in the title of your document. If you don't want anything to appear in one of the prompts, click on it and press the **Delete** key on your keyboard.

To move from the header to the footer, click on the **Go to Footer** button, in the 'Navigation' group. Select a style from the drop-down list that appears.

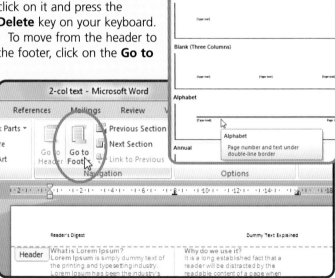

Customising Word

Change your preferences

Word comes with predefined settings suitable for general word processing use. However, you can change these settings if you feel that others would be more useful. For example, if the ruler at the top of the screen measures in inches but you prefer to work in centimetres, it is a simple matter of changing the measurement setting to your choice.

SEE ALSO...
- *Spelling and grammar* p58
- *AutoCorrect your text* p62

YOUR CHOICE

Click on the Office button, then on Word Options. Here, you can customise common tasks, such as editing, saving and printing your work, so that they are carried out automatically in the way you prefer.

Viewing options

You will see a list of preference options in the left-hand pane, split into two sections. You will need to change some preferences more than others. Click on **Display** in the left pane. The right pane is divided into three sections, with options that allow you to alter how a page is displayed on screen, and how it will print. Clicking on any box adds a tick, which means that particular option has been selected.

The uppermost section, 'Page display options', allows you to select whether to see screen items such as highlighter marks and tooltips.

The next section, 'Always show these formatting marks on the screen' lets you determine whether items such as tab characters, paragraph marks and object anchors are shown. These can be useful when laying out documents and it is a good idea to tick the **Show all formatting marks** box.

'Printing options' determine which formatting objects are printed from your document.

Display options

Click on **Advanced** in the left pane, and the right pane is now divided into 10 sections. Scroll down to the 'Display' section. Here you can change measurement units from inches to centimetres or millimetres, or the typesetting measurements from points to picas. You can also

Watch out

Beware of the save option 'Always create backup copy'. You could end up with lots of copies of the same file piling up on your hard disk, so make sure you delete them regularly. For long-term file backups, always save to another disk, such as a CD or DVD.

choose how many entries you want to show in the 'Recent documents list', which appears when you click on the Office button. This provides you with a quick way of opening a document that you have recently worked on.

Editing options

Editing functions, such as selecting, cutting and pasting text and styling paragraphs, can all be

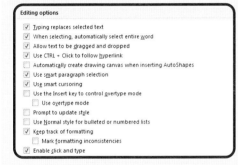

modified in this section. For instance, if you select 'Allow text to be dragged and dropped', you can highlight text in your document, then just click and drag it to place it somewhere else. If you select 'Enable click and type', you can position your cursor anywhere in your document and start typing. Click 'Use smart cursoring' for spaces to be added or removed as necessary when you move text around.

Printing and saving

If you find that you regularly have to change the setup in Print dialogue boxes, or you have to save and make backups when working in Word, it may be more efficient to set your printing and

saving preferences here. For instance, you can save on ink if you print out all your documents as 'Draft', selecting a higher quality only for letters and other important items.

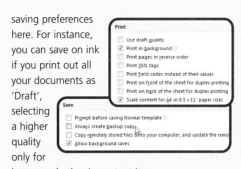

Proofing preferences

Click on **Proofing** in the left pane and in the sections in the right pane, you can specify various spelling and grammar rules. Some of the options displayed apply to all Office programs. You can specify whether you want Word to indicate spelling or grammar errors as you type. You can also select a UK dictionary or another language dictionary to check your spelling.

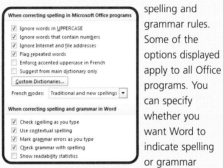

File locations

When you save a document, Word anticipates where you will wish to save it. For instance, you might save your documents into the 'Documents' folder. You can change these locations by clicking

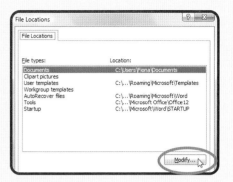

the **Modify** button and selecting folders for the different file types.

Compatibility preferences

If you need to create a document that someone will open in a different word processing program, click on the drop-down arrow next to 'Lay out this document as if created in' and select the appropriate program. To specify your own settings, click on **Custom**. In the 'Layout Options' panel, Word selects the layout choices it recommends for this document.

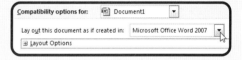

User information preferences

Each time a document is saved, user information is added to the file properties, such as the name of the person who created that document and their initials. Click on **Popular** in the left pane and update that information in the right pane.

Close up
Using the 'Proofing' options, under 'When correcting spelling and grammar in Word', you can override a previous spelling check, and re-check a document – for instance, if you do not want your grammar checked as you work.

The Quick Access Toolbar

Traditionally, Microsoft Office programs contained numerous toolbars with rows of buttons that you clicked on to perform commands. In Microsoft Office 2007 most of these toolbars have been replaced by the Ribbon, where buttons are grouped together for easy access. Additionally, there is a customisable 'Quick Access Toolbar' to display your most popular commands.

SEE ALSO...

● Explore the program p16

BEFORE YOU START
Situated to the right of the Microsoft 'Office' button is the Quick Access Toolbar. By default, this toolbar displays 3 buttons, 'Save', 'Undo' and 'Repeat' or 'Redo'.

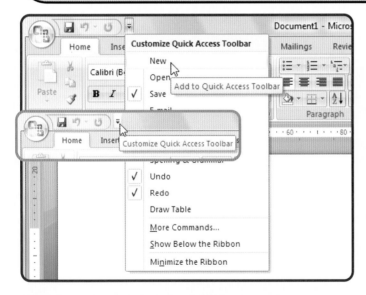

1 You can customise the Quick Access Toolbar to add buttons for the commands you use most often. Click on the **Customize Quick Access Toolbar** button to the right of the Quick Launch Toolbar to display a list of options. Commands already selected have a 'tick' next to them. Click on additional commands to add these buttons to the toolbar. If you wish to delete an option, simply click on it and the button is removed.

2 Click on **More Commands** to see a full list of available commands. Click on the commands you want in the list on the left, then on **Add** to add them to the list on the right. To delete commands no longer required, click on them in the list on the right, then on **Remove**. When you have finished, click on **OK**.

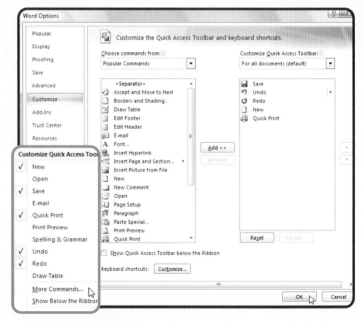

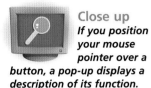

Close up
If you position your mouse pointer over a button, a pop-up displays a description of its function.

Close up
You can also access the 'Customize Quick Access Toolbar' options by clicking the Office button, then Word Options and then selecting Customize *from the pane on the left.*

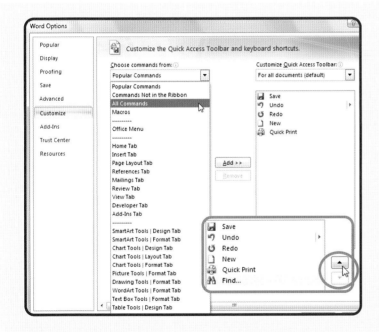

3 Alternatively, in the 'Choose commands from' panel click on the drop-down list and select from the options, which are grouped by category.

You can also change the location of a button on the toolbar by clicking on it in the right pane, and then clicking on the **Up** or **Down** arrows on the right.

4 You can save this new version of the toolbar for all your documents, or the current document only.

Select the appropriate option from the drop-down list in the 'Customize Quick Access Toolbar' panel and click **OK**.

Viewing options

There are several different ways of viewing a document on your screen. If you are designing a poster, making a brochure or writing a letter, you will probably want to see what it will look like when it is printed or published. Having an overview of the document will also make it easier to restructure it. Find out how Word's options can make your work easier on the eyes.

SEE ALSO...
● *Print your work* p24

CHOOSING YOUR VIEW

All views are accessed by clicking on the 'View' tab and selecting from the 'Document Views' group. 'Print Layout' is the first option and probably the one you will use the most for creating, editing and styling your documents. There are, however, several alternatives for viewing documents on screen.

Full Screen Reading

Use this view to make your documents more legible on screen. Although the same fonts are used, a special technology called 'ClearType'

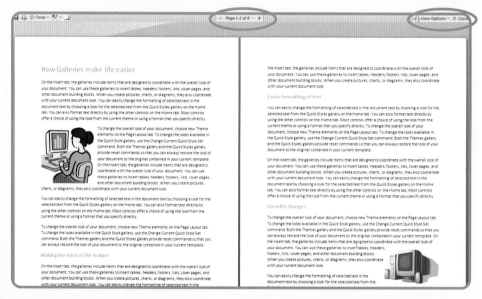

makes the text much easier on the eyes. This view is useful for reading long documents with a lot of dense text.

In this view the Ribbon is hidden to maximise the viewing area. At the top centre of the screen is a page indicator showing the current page number

Close up
All of the 'Viewing Options' described in these pages are to be found within the 5 groups (Document Views, Show/Hide, Zoom and Window) of the View tab.

and the total number of pages. It also has a pop-up menu containing other navigational controls. On either side of the page numbers are arrow buttons to move forwards and backwards through the document.

You can customise this view by clicking on the **View Options** button in the top right corner of the screen and then selecting from the drop-down list of options. To close the Full Screen Reading View, click on the **Close** button located at the top right of the screen.

Web Layout
This view enables you to see what your document would look like if viewed as a web page in Internet Explorer.

Outline
This structural overview is useful as it shows different levels of headings and subheadings within a document. The controls allow you to move between the levels, repositioning lines or collapsing them so that headings or subheadings on lower levels are hidden temporarily.

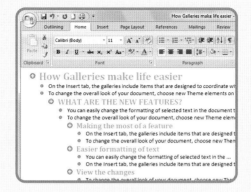

You can write, select, edit and style all your headings at once, or individually. To restructure the entire document, click on the symbol to the left of a heading, and drag it to a new position.

Draft
In 'Draft' view your document is displayed in a simplified manner, with headers, footers and images not visible. You can edit your text, but to see how the document will look when printed, you will need to view it in 'Print Layout' view.

Print Layout
Probably the most useful and most used view of the group, Print Layout allows you to create, edit and then view your document as it will appear when printed. The complete page is displayed, including margins, headers and footers, columns, and any images you have added, all of which are positioned correctly on screen.

This mode of working is often referred to as working in 'WYSIWYG' format, which means 'What You See Is What You Get'.

Document Map
The Document Map creates a structured list of the headings used in your document within a pane located on the left of the main page area. Click on **Document Map** in the 'Show/Hide'

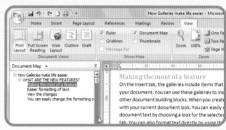

group to select it. This is a useful feature for navigating through a long document. The left pane has its own scroll bars which let you scroll through the headings and subheadings. When you select a heading in this pane the main page area will move to that line.

To close this view either click on the 'X' at the top right of the left pane or click on **Document Map** again in the 'Show/Hide' group to deselect it.

Thumbnails
Another way of browsing your document is to use the left pane to display small thumbnail images of each page. Click on **Thumbnails** in the 'Show/Hide' group to activate this viewing option.

In the Thumbnails pane, click on a thumbnail to move straight to that page in the main window. To increase the

Bright idea
All of the views described above can be accessed from the Status bar positioned at the bottom right of a window.

Close up
Headings and subheadings shown in the left pane are in a 'tree' structure. If you click on the '–' in the left pane, the subheadings beneath this line are collapsed and the icon changes to a '+'. If you click on this the subheadings will reappear.

width of the left pane so that you can view more thumbnails, click and drag on the border between the two areas.

To close this view and remove the pane, you can either click on the 'X' at the top right of the left pane or click on Thumbnails in the 'Show/Hide' group to deselect this option.

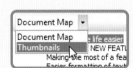

Zoom

In the 'Zoom' group of the 'View' tab there are various options to let you resize the view of your document. You can zoom to 100%, scale your document so that a single page fits the width of your window,

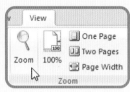

scale it so that two pages fit the window, or scale it so that the page width occupies the total width of the window.

Click on the **Zoom** button and select from the pre-set options. If you click on the **Many pages** button, a drop-down list displays a grid of display

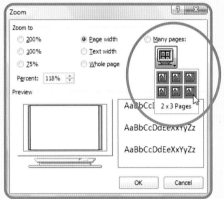

options. Move your mouse pointer over the page icons to select one of these. Click on **OK** to apply the Zoom setting. Alternatively, click on **Text width**, for example, to make the text as large as possible without the need for horizontal scrolling.

Using multiple windows

Occasionally it can be useful to view a document in several windows at the same time, so you can zoom or scroll differently in each window. You may also want to have several documents on the screen at the same time, to copy and paste from one document to another, for example.

Click on **New Window** and a second window will open in front of the first, so you now have two windows containing the same document. Click on **Arrange All** to position the windows so that they are both visible one above the other.

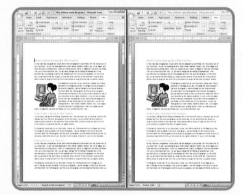

Then click on **View Side by Side** to view one next to the other.

To switch to another open window, click on **Switch Windows** and select it from the drop-down list.

Watch out
The 'Document Map' and the 'Thumbnails' features both use the same left pane of the screen, so only one can be selected at any time.

Using Graphics

Add a picture

Inserting graphics or pictures into a document can instantly add impact and clarity to your subject. You can either use your own pictures, or choose from the vast gallery of ClipArt provided by Word. Desktop publishing is also made easy by allowing you to integrate illustrations and charts with your text, to produce professional-looking results.

SEE ALSO...
- *Create a family newsletter* p80
- *WordArt & AutoShapes* p84
- *Add a background* p86

BEFORE YOU START
Open a document. You may already have a picture that you want to insert but don't worry if you haven't – you can easily find graphics stored on your computer, on a CD or on the Internet.

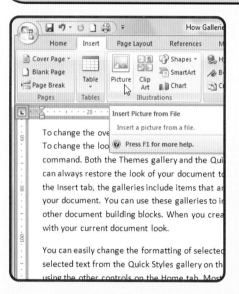

1 To add a graphic to your document, first position the cursor where you would like to insert the image. Next, go to the **Insert** tab and select **Picture** from the 'Illustrations' group. Use this to insert an image stored on your PC, a CD-ROM or other removeable storage device.

2 The Insert Picture dialogue box appears on screen. It automatically shows your 'Pictures' folder, where you will see some sample images. Click on the drop-down list in the 'Look in' panel to browse for your image file.

Click on **Views** on the Menu bar to select the best viewing options for your pictures. Click on a picture to select it, then on **Insert**.

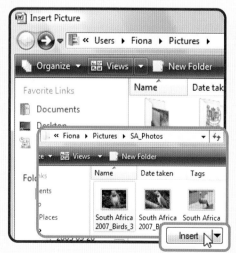

3 Alternatively, to insert a picture from Word's Clip Gallery, go to the **Insert** tab and choose **Clip Art** from the 'Illustrations' group. The Clip Art Task Pane appears. Type a keyword into the 'Search for' panel. Then select where you want to search in the 'Search in' panel.

Text-Wrapping

You can wrap the text around the graphic in different ways. Click on **Text Wrapping** in the 'Arrange' group, scroll down the list and click on a style to select it.

Watch out

Although it is fine to use ClipArt in documents such as newsletters and flyers, it is not legal to use it for promotional or marketing material, nor can you publish a document containing it.

4 Now click on the **Go** button next to your keyword. Your results will be displayed as thumbnails in the panel below. Hover your mouse over a thumbnail for information on that image. Select your choice of picture and then click on **Insert**.

5 If you have an Internet connection click on **Clip art on Office Online** for a greater selection of images. In the Microsoft Office Online website, type your keyword into the search bar and click on **Search**. Add a tick to select images, then click on **Download**, and follow the prompts.

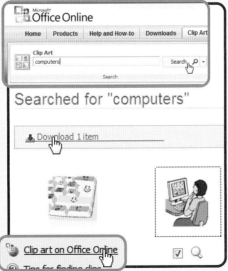

the Quick Style command. Bot provide reset of your docum template. On 1 designed to co You can use th cover pages, a ures, charts, or diagrams, they also co

6 To resize an image, click on it, then click and drag on a handle (above). Use the controls in the 'Adjust' group to adjust brightness, contrast and colours. Right-click on the image and choose **Edit Picture**. You can now select individual elements and edit them. Experiment to achieve different effects.

Create a party invite

Making your own invitation allows you to create a design that reflects the type of event you are organising – and the type of person you are arranging it for. If it is going to be a lively party, use bright colours and fun fonts. If it is for a formal dinner party, you can choose more subtle colours and traditional fonts.

SEE ALSO...
- *Add a picture* p74
- *WordArt and AutoShapes* p84
- *Add a background* p86

BEFORE YOU START
Open a new A4 document, name it and save it. Go to the **Page Layout** tab and click on *Margins* in the 'Page Setup' group. Click on *Custom Margins*, set 'Top' and 'Bottom' to *0cm*. Click **OK**, then on **Fix** and **OK** again.

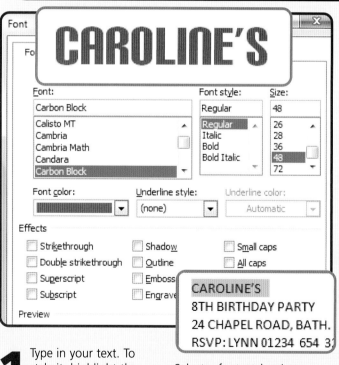

1 Type in your text. To style it, highlight the first part, click on the **Font** dialogue box launcher and click on the **Font** tab.

Select a font, style, size, colour and effect, then click **OK**. Continue to style the rest of your text in a similar way.

2 Highlight all your text and click on the **Center** button, found in the 'Paragraph' group. For special effects you can use WordArt – a gallery containing a selection of text designs that you can edit and customise. Highlight the text you want to add an effect to and click on **Cut** in the 'Clipboard' group.

Expert advice
You can exaggerate the effect of the WordArt shape by clicking on the yellow diamond and dragging it across the screen.

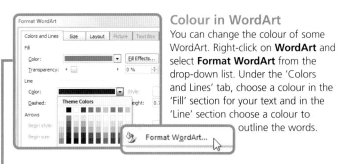

Colour in WordArt
You can change the colour of some WordArt. Right-click on **WordArt** and select **Format WordArt** from the drop-down list. Under the 'Colors and Lines' tab, choose a colour in the 'Fill' section for your text and in the 'Line' section choose a colour to outline the words.

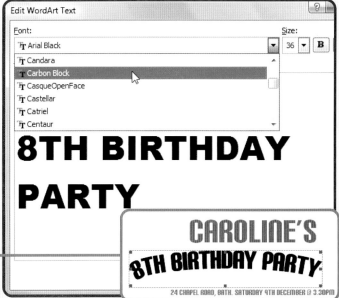

4 In the Edit WordArt dialogue box select a font, size and style for your WordArt text, then click **OK**. Your text will now appear in the document in your chosen style. To select a colour, right-click on the WordArt box and click **Format WordArt**. In the dialogue box, select from the 'Color' drop-down list.

3 Go to the **Insert** tab and click on **WordArt** in the 'Text' group. Then click on a style in the WordArt Gallery. The Edit WordArt Text dialogue box appears displaying [Your Text Here] in the 'Text' box. Hold down the **Ctrl** key then press the '**V**' key to paste in your text. Click on **OK**.

Letterspacing in WordArt

You can adjust the spacing between WordArt

letters, or characters. With your WordArt selected, click on the **Spacing** button in the 'Text' group, then on one of the spacing options in the pop-up menu.

You can exaggerate the effect of the WordArt shape by clicking on the yellow diamond shape handle and dragging it across the screen.

6 With your WordArt selected, use your cursor keys to move it, so it sits neatly between the first and third lines. To adjust the shape of your WordArt, click on it,

then click on the **WordArt Shape** button in the 'WordArt Styles' group. A palette will then pop up offering you a selection of effects. Click on your choice.

5 With your WordArt selected, click on the **Center** button in the 'Paragraph' group. Now roughly space out your lines of text by pressing the **Enter** key. Select your WordArt again, go to the **Format** tab, select **Text Wrapping**, then **In Front of Text**.

Bright idea
For a professional look, print your invitations on card. Not all printers can handle card, however, so you may need to copy the document onto a CD/DVD and take it to a print shop.

8 Now go to the 'Arrange' group and click on **Text Wrapping** and then on **Behind Text**. Your text will automatically move back onto the first page and sit neatly in front of your picture. To print out the invitation, go to the **Office** button and select **Print** from the left pane.

7 If you wish, you can add a photograph to your invitation. Position your cursor at the top of the page. Go to the **Insert** tab and click on **Picture** in the 'Insert' group. In the dialogue box, navigate to your picture, click on it, then on **Insert**. Your text will automatically move down to create space for the new image.

Create a family newsletter

One of the best ways to keep family members in touch, no matter how far apart they are, is by compiling a regular newsletter. The first task is to ask your relatives whether they would like to contribute any news, such as a new job or a recently passed exam or favourite recipes. Word makes it easy by providing you with templates that are easy to adapt.

SEE ALSO...
- *Using columns* p38
- *Spelling and grammar* p58

BEFORE YOU START
Go to the **Office** button and click on **New**. Scroll down the list of templates on the left and click on **Newsletters**. In the middle pane select a style, here 'Family newsletter', and click on **Download**.

1 Your downloaded newsletter template will appear with 'dummy' text in place and pictures already positioned for you to replace with your own. This template style is already pre-formatted into two columns which contain text and picture boxes ready for you to start creating your own newsletter.

2 Highlight the prompt 'Newsletter Date' and type in a date or season. Then highlight the heading of the first article, and type in a new one. Next highlight the body of the first article and type in the story. Don't worry if your story is shorter or longer than the default as you can adjust the text box later (see page 83).

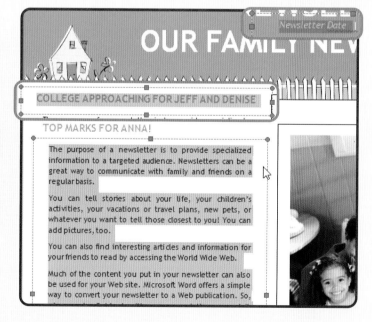

Close up
To use photographs in your newsletter, scan them in or download them from a digital camera and save them on your PC. Go to the Insert *menu, select* Picture *then click on* From File. *Find your photograph and click on* Insert.

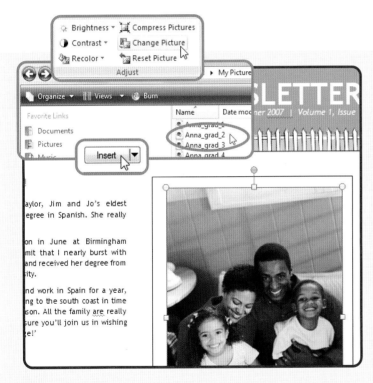

3 Replace the default photograph with one of your own, to match the story. Double-click on the photograph in column two of the newsletter and in the 'Adjust' group click on **Change Picture**. Navigate to the folder containing your photographs and click on one to select it. Then click on Insert.

4 Highlight and replace the caption text. Then click inside the caption text box and when the mouse pointer changes into a cross shape, click and drag the caption box to the required position. Click on the ruled box around the picture and caption to select it, then click and drag one of the 'square' blue handles to resize it.

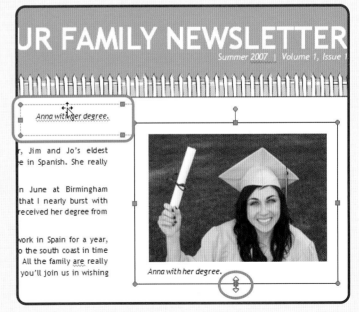

Bright idea
For a professional look, style all your headings using the same font, font style and font size. Use colour only for headings as coloured text can be difficult to read.

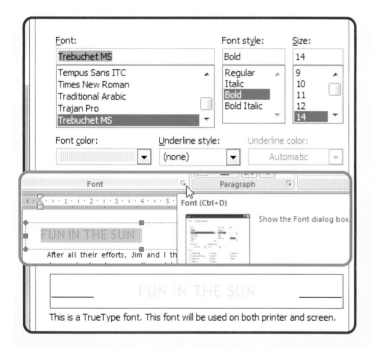

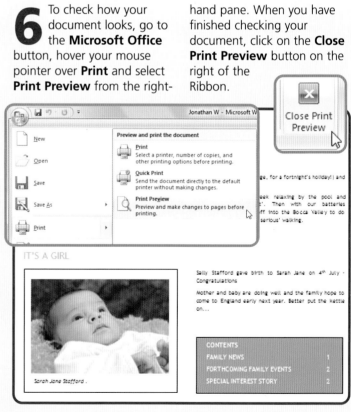

6 To check how your document looks, go to the **Microsoft Office** button, hover your mouse pointer over **Print** and select **Print Preview** from the right- hand pane. When you have finished checking your document, click on the **Close Print Preview** button on the right of the Ribbon.

5 Highlight the heading of one of your articles, and click on the **Font** dialogue box launcher. Select a font, font style and size. If you are printing in colour, click on the arrow next to the 'Font color' panel, scroll down and select a colour. Click on **OK**. Repeat for the other headings.

Adjusting text boxes

All text boxes have eight handles – a round handle at each corner and a square handle on each side. To adjust the size of a text box, simply click and hold your mouse pointer over one of the square handles until it changes to a double-headed arrow. Click and drag on the handle and a dotted line will show the new size. Release the mouse to keep those dimensions.

bags (such a lot of luggage, for a fortnight's holiday!) and headed for the sun.

We spent our first week relaxing by the pool and generally 'chilling out'. Then with our batteries recharged we headed off into the Bocca Valley to do some bird watching and 'serious' walking.

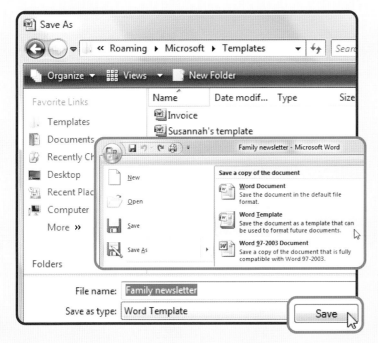

7 To save your newsletter as a template, click on the **Microsoft Office** button, hover your mouse over **Save As** and select **Word Template** from the right-hand pane. Click on **Templates** in the left-hand pane of the Save As dialogue box. Name your template and click on **Save**.

8 As an alternative to printing out and then distributing your newsletter to family and friends by hand, send it out to them as an e-mail attachment. To do this, click on the **Microsoft Office** button, hover your mouse over **Send** and select **E-mail**. This will open an e-mail message with your newsletter attached and the 'Subject' line filled in. Add the recipients and a message, then send it.

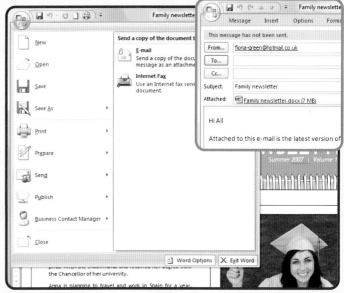

WordArt and AutoShapes

You can make text behave like a graphic image if you use WordArt. Just pick one of the predefined styles and type in the word you wish to use. You can then reshape and resize it, and wrap normal text around it. AutoShapes are graphics such as stars, arrows and smiley faces. You can add them to your document, and position and size them to suit your page.

SEE ALSO...
- *Add a picture* p74
- *Create a party invite* p76

BEFORE YOU START
*Create a new blank document. Go to the **Microsoft Office** button and click on **New**, then **Blank document**. Alternatively, click on **Open** in the Office menu to open an existing file.*

USING WORDART

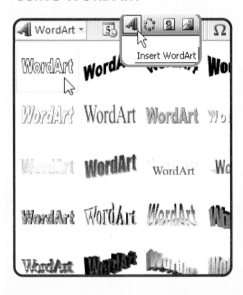

1 To insert WordArt into your document, click on the page roughly where you want your WordArt text to appear. Click on the **Insert** tab, then on **WordArt** in the 'Text' group. Choose a style and click the **Insert WordArt** button on the toolbar.

2 The Edit WordArt Text dialogue box appears, with the words 'Your Text Here' highlighted. Type your own words over them. Use the 'Font' and 'Size' panels, and the 'Bold' and 'Italic' buttons at the top of the dialogue box to style your text. When you are happy with the styling, click on **OK** to view the WordArt in your document.

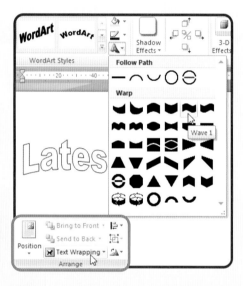

3 With the WordArt selected, you can move and resize it like an image (see page 74). The Ribbon automatically displays the relevant tools to assist you in formatting your WordArt text. You can edit your words, change the style and shape of your graphic and choose how text on the page wraps around it.

Arranging graphics

The Drawing Tools automatically appear on the Ribbon when a graphic image is selected. These commands are organised within groups. In the 'Arrange' group, for example, click on **Text Wrapping** to choose how your graphic and text interact on the page. Click on **Position** and move your cursor over the pre-set images to preview the effect.

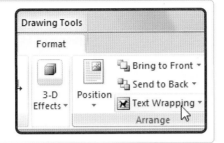

That's amazing!
You can even add text to an AutoShape. Right-click on the shape and choose **Add Text** from the pop-up menu. All you have to do is type in the text and it will wrap automatically inside the AutoShape.

USING AUTOSHAPES

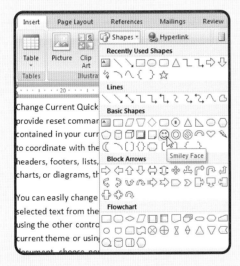

1 To insert an AutoShape into your document, go to the **Insert** tab and click on **Shapes** in the 'Illustrations' group. A drop-down list of shapes, categorised into groups, will appear on screen. Hover your mouse pointer over a shape for a pop-up description of it.

2 In the 'Basic Shapes' category click on **Smiley Face**. Your mouse pointer now changes shape to a cross-hair. Click and drag in your document to create an outline shape. The width to height ratio will be preserved if you hold down the **Shift** key while dragging. To re-size the shape, hold the pointer over a round handle until it changes to a double-headed arrow. Then click and drag to your new size.

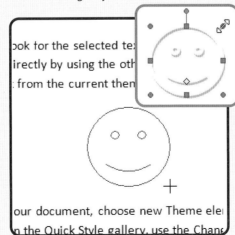

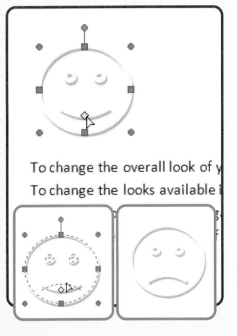

3 To change the Smiley Face to a Sad Face, select it, then click on the yellow diamond in the centre of the mouth and drag it up, so that the corners of the mouth turn down.

Add a background

Giving your document a coloured or textured background is a great way to liven it up. You can write over the top and insert picture and text boxes. Although you cannot print Word's 'Backgrounds', the 'Watermark' function allows you to print a faded version, which is ideal for creating stylish personalised stationery.

SEE ALSO...
- Design a letterhead *p42*
- Headers and footers *p52*
- Add a picture *p74*

BACKGROUNDS

Use the 'Background' feature to create coloured and textured pages for files that you don't need to print out.

With your document open, go to the **Page Layout** tab and click on **Page Color** in the 'Page Background' group. To add a solid colour to your document, just select one from the colours displayed. If you don't see the shade you want, click **More Colors**. For two tones, patterns and pictures, click on **Fill Effects**. Select the **Gradient**

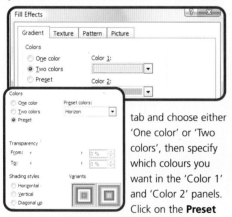

tab and choose either 'One color' or 'Two colors', then specify which colours you want in the 'Color 1' and 'Color 2' panels. Click on the **Preset** option to view different themes such as 'Desert' or 'Rainbow'. 'Shading styles' changes the way the two colours are mixed. View 'Variants' on the right and double-click to select a background.

For other options, click on the **Texture** tab and choose a pre-set background or click the **Pattern** tab and select a colour from the 'Foreground' and 'Background' panels, then double-click on a pattern box to select it.

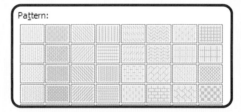

If you want to insert an image file as your page background, click the **Picture** tab, then **Select Picture**. A dialogue box will open which lists all the images stored in your 'Pictures' folder. Select a picture, click **Insert**, then click **OK**.

WATERMARKS

Word's 'Watermark' feature places a faded version of your chosen graphic on the page, which can be printed.

Go to the **Page Layout** tab and click on **Watermark** in the 'Page Background' group. Click on **Custom Watermark** in the drop-down list. In the Printed Watermark dialogue box you can select either a picture or text watermark. To insert a picture, click on **Picture watermark**,

then on **Select Picture**. Images stored in your 'Pictures' folder are listed. Select a picture and click on **Insert**. Select a scale to size the watermark or leave at 'Auto' to fit the image to the margins. If your watermark is very pale, tick the 'washout' box, then click **OK**. Any text that you type will appear in front of the watermark.

If you want to use text for your watermark, select from the pre-set options or click on **Custom watermark**. Click on **Text watermark**, key your text into the 'Text' panel, then select a font, size, colour and orientation (diagonal or horizontal), and then click on **OK**.

Special Functions

Mail Merge

When you need to send the same letter to lots of people, the mail merge facility is a fantastic time saver. You can create one letter and merge it with a data file of all the relevant names and addresses. You can use this feature for all kinds of mass mailings, whether you're writing to family and friends, club members or business contacts.

SEE ALSO...
- *Make address labels* p90
- *Use macros* p94

BEFORE YOU START
You may wish to use data such as names and addresses from Microsoft Outlook, but you can also create a new data source while setting up the mail merge (see page 90).

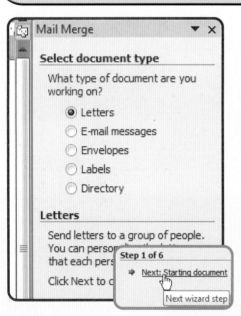

2 In Step 2, under 'Select starting document' choose one of the three options. For example, choose **Use the current document** if you are happy to type the content of your letter in the current document. Alternatively, you can use a template or another existing document. Then click on **Next: Select recipients**.

1 Open a new document, go to the **Mailings** tab and in the 'Start Mail Merge' group, click on **Start Mail Merge**. Select **Step by Step Mail Merge Wizard**. In the Task Pane under 'Select document type' choose **Letters**. Then click **Next: Starting document**.

3 Under 'Select recipients' choose from the three options displayed for a source list of your recipients. Click **Choose Contacts Folder**, then in the Choose Profile dialogue box, select your profile, and click **OK**. In the Select Contacts dialogue box, select your contact folder, and click **OK**. The Mail Merge Recipients dialogue box displays your list. Edit it if necessary and click **OK**. Select **Next: Write your letter**.

That's amazing!
Use Mail Merge to print addresses directly onto envelopes. In Step 1, select **Envelopes**, then click on **Next** and then on **Envelope options** to choose the size and orientation of your envelope. Click **OK** and then **Next**. Follow the remaining steps, selecting from options as directed. Finally click **Next: Complete the merge** to finish.

Close up
You may need to alter some field names. Take time to think about those relevant to your own data, removing any you do not want, typing over and adding others, and leave an extra one, which you can edit later.

Bright idea
Always check your work before you print. The 'Preview your letters' feature in Step 5 lets you check what your letters will look like to save you wasting paper.

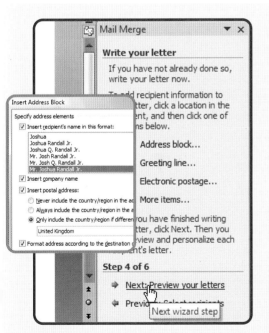

5 Under 'Preview your letters' you can see how your letters will look before you print them. You can make further changes to your recipient list by clicking on 'Edit recipient list' under 'Make changes'.

Finally, select **Next: Complete the merge**.

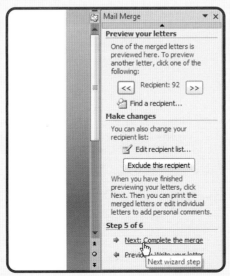

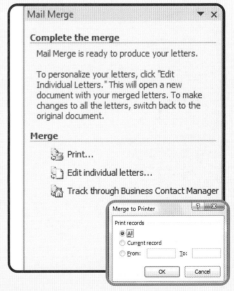

4 Customise your letter with a standard address block or greeting line by clicking on the options under 'Write your letter'.

When you have finished, click on **Next: Preview your letters**.

6 You can personalise your letters by clicking **Edit individual letters** under 'Merge'. This will open a new document for your merged letters.

Alternatively, click 'Print' and make your choices in the Merge to Printer dialogue box. Finally click **OK**, then **OK** again to print the letters.

Make address labels

Addressing numerous envelopes is a repetitive and time-consuming task. However, Word's label printing feature can save you a lot of effort and makes your envelopes look professional. If you already have address lists stored on your PC, you can use the merge feature to print the details as labels, or create sheets of address labels for individual contacts.

SEE ALSO...
- *Templates* p50
- *Mail Merge* p88

BEFORE YOU START
Open a blank Word document, name it and save it. You may have an address list already, but don't worry if you haven't – we'll show you how to do this with the Mail Merge Wizard.

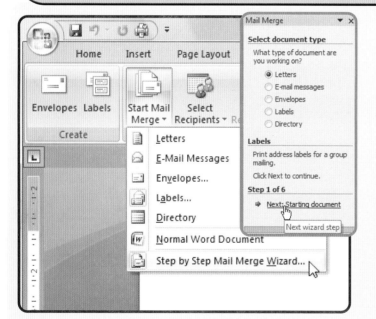

1 Go to the **Mailings** tab and in the 'Start Mail Merge' group, click on **Start Mail Merge**. From the drop-down list select **Step by Step Mail Merge Wizard**. In the Mail Merge task pane choose **Labels** under 'Select document type'. Then click **Next: Starting document** to go to the following step of the wizard.

2 Under 'Select starting document' choose whether you want to change the document layout or start from the existing document. Here we've selected **Change document layout**. Now under 'Change document layout' click on **Label options** and select your label size.

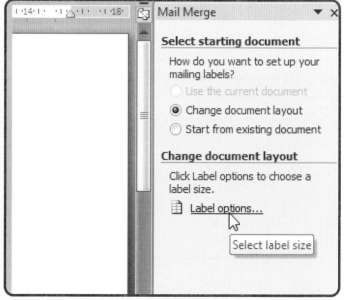

New label

If your label type is not listed, you will need to enter the details. In the Label Options dialogue box, click on the **New Label** button, add the label dimensions and then give your label a name. Finally, click **OK**.

Key word
A field marks a place in your document. When you perform a merge, the fields instruct your program where to put the information you're merging into your document, such as names and addresses.

Close up
Sheets of address labels come in various sizes. Each page size and configuration of labels has its own reference number. For A4 printers, one of the most popular is the L7163, with 14 labels on an A4 sheet.

Label Options

Printer information
- ○ Continuous-feed printers
- ● Page printers   Tray: Default tray (Automatic) ▼

Label information

Label vendors: Avery A4/A5 ▼

Product number:
- L7163
- L7163X
- L7164
- L7165
- L7165X
- L7166

Label information
- Type: Ad
- Height: 3.
- Width: 9.
- Page size: 21

[Details...] [New Label...] [Delete]

4 Your original blank document now displays a grid of blank labels set out in columns and rows to the match the specifications of your labels. Click **Next: Select recipients** to continue to the next step in the wizard.

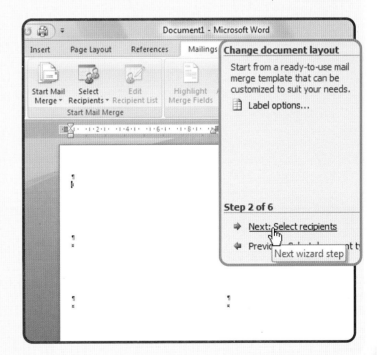

3 In the Label Options dialogue box select the manufacturer of your labels from the 'Label vendors' drop-down list and choose the correct label number from the 'Product number' drop-down list. Click **OK**. Alternatively, click on the **New Label** button (see instructions above). When you have finished, click **OK**.

Expert advice
To print a one-off label, or a whole sheet of the same address, go to the **Mailings** tab and select **Labels** in the 'Create' group. With the 'Labels' tab selected, type your information into the 'Address' panel. Click the **Options** button, select your label type and click **OK**. Now opt to print a full page of the same label, or single label. Click **Print**.

6 In the Save Address List dialogue box enter a name for your list and click on **Save**. The Mail Merge Recipients dialogue box will then appear. Check that the details of your list are correct, make any necessary adjustments and click **OK**.
At the bottom of the pane click **Next: Arrange your labels** for the next step.

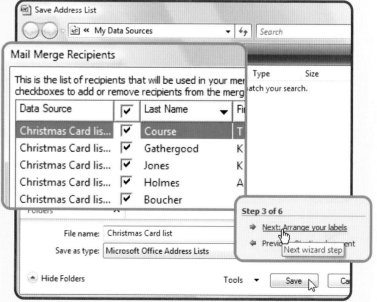

5 Under 'Select recipients' you can choose to 'Use an existing list', 'Select from Outlook contacts' or 'Type a new list', if you don't already have one. If you choose to generate a new list, click on **Create**. The New Address List dialogue box appears. Fill in the fields for your first recipient, then click **New Entry** to add another. When you have finished, click **OK**.

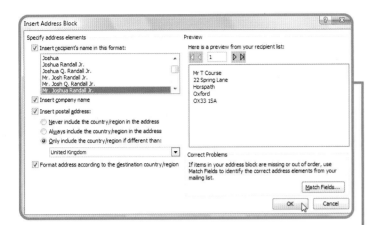

Watch out
Before you print the whole list of address labels, it's a good idea to do a test run on plain paper. You only need to print out one page of addresses to check that it is laid out as you want. To do this, click on **Pages** under the 'Page range' section in the Print dialogue box, and type '1' in the panel beside it. Click **OK**. Only your first page of labels will print.

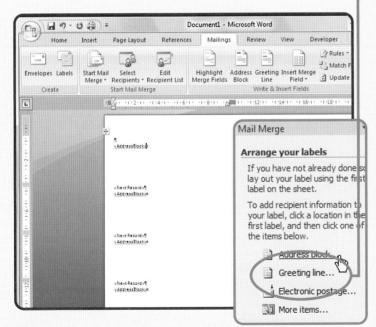

8 Check your labels and make any adjustments. Click **Next: Complete the merge**, then **Print**. The Merge to Printer dialogue box appears. Check your 'Print records' settings and click **OK**. Click **OK** again to print.

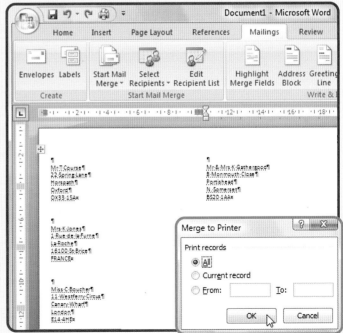

7 You can lay out your label by adding items such as an address block to the first label. Click on Address block under 'Arrange your labels'. In the Insert Address Block dialogue box choose your address elements and check your results in the 'Preview' pane. Click **OK**. Then click **Next: Preview your labels**.

Use Macros

If you have a particular piece of text or an item, such as a table, that you often use in documents, it makes sense to save it as a macro, instead of creating it from scratch each time. Whenever you wish to add that item to a page, simply run your macro. A macro can be assigned to a button on the Quick Access Toolbar or to a combination of keystrokes.

SEE ALSO...
● *Design a letterhead* p42
● *The Quick Access Toolbar* p68

BEFORE YOU START
Decide exactly what you want to save as a macro and how you want it to look, whether it is your name and address or a table with a specific number of rows and columns.

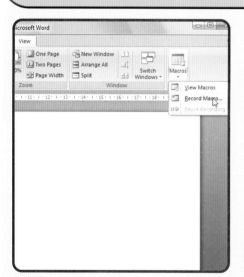

2 In the 'Macro name' panel, give your macro a name, choosing something that reminds you of its function. Under 'Store macro in' you can select 'All Documents' to save your macro in Word's blank document template, or just add it to the document you're currently working on.
To assign your macro to a button or to create a keyboard shortcut for it, click on either the **Button** or the **Keyboard** icon, as appropriate.

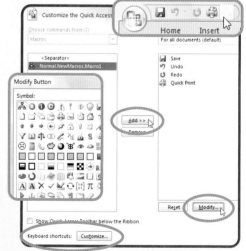

1 To create a macro you need to record all of the instructions you would normally use when you are creating your chosen item. These can then be played back instantly, at any time, to recreate it. Go to the **View** tab and click on **Macros** and then on **Record Macro**. The Record Macro dialogue box will appear on screen.

3 If you clicked on the **Button** icon, you'll see the macro under 'Choose commands from'. Click on it and then on **Add** to add it to the Quick Access Toolbar. To assign a button to it, click **Modify**, select a symbol, then click **OK**.
To create a keyboard command for your macro as well, click the **Customize** button next to 'Keyboard shortcuts'. Otherwise, click on **Close**.

Editing Macros

If you want to change some of the text contained in a macro, go to the **Macros** tab and click on **Macro**. Choose the relevant macro and click the **Edit** button. Any text shown in quotation marks can be highlighted and typed over, as normal.

If you wish to change commands in your macro, it is best to delete your macro and recreate it from scratch.

Watch out

Macros can be used to spread computer viruses, so if you open a file created by someone else and a dialogue box appears, asking whether you want to enable macros, the file could have a virus. The safest option is to not enable the macro and to check the file with your anti-virus software before you open it.

4 In the Customize Keyboard dialogue box, type a keyboard command that will activate your macro into the 'Press new shortcut key' panel – **Alt + Ctrl + Shift + A**, for example. You can see below whether this command is assigned to another function. If it is not, click the **Assign** button, then **Close**. Then click **OK**.

5 The Macro toolbar appears on screen. It is very small and has two buttons – click the left button to stop recording and the right button to pause. Click again on the right button to resume recording.

Create the item that you wish to include in your macro. When it looks exactly how you want it, click on the **Stop Recording** button.

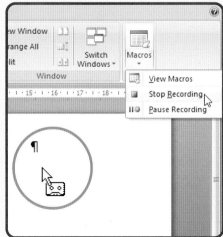

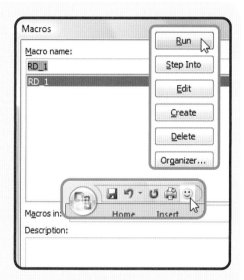

6 The next time you want to add that item to a document, click on the toolbar button or menu to which you assigned your macro, or press your keyboard command.

Alternatively, go to the **Macros** tab and click on **View Macros**. In the dialogue box is a list of available macros. Click on your macro and select **Run**.

Sort a list

Word enables you to sort information contained in lists or tables. For example, you may want to make a list of the members of your local club and sort it alphabetically by name. You can also sort by date or number in ascending or descending order, but you need to ensure that you have defined and identified the criteria and format for your sort.

SEE ALSO...

● *Using tables* p48

BEFORE YOU START
Be aware that if you type a space at the beginning of a word, it will *appear first in the list, as a space comes before 'A' in the alphabet, as do punctuation, symbols or numbers.*

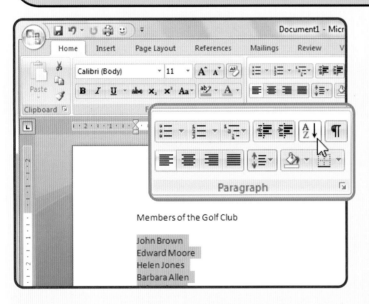

2 To sort your list by the last name, click the **Options** button. Under 'Separate fields at', select the **Other** option and type a space in the panel to the right. Then click on **OK**. In the Sort Text dialogue box, click on the drop-down list below 'Sort by' and select **Word 2**.

Ensure **Text** is chosen in the 'Type' panel. Click **OK** to start the sort.

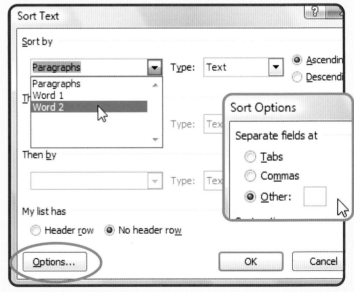

1 To sort a list of names alphabetically, type in the first names followed by the last names in any order. Press the **Return** key after each entry. When the list is complete, highlight it, and click on the Home tab. In the 'Paragraph' group click on the **Sort** button. In the Sort Text dialogue box that appears, the default setting is to sort your list from A to Z (Ascending), by the first word of each entry. If this is what you want, click **OK**.

Bright idea
For easier sorting, convert a list to a table. Highlight the list, go to the Insert *tab, click on* Table*, then* Convert Text to Table*. Use the options in the dialogue box to format the table and specify how entries should be separated into cells.*

Watch out
If you want to sort a mixed list by numbers, make sure you specify Number in the 'Type' panel, so that the sort function ignores everything in the list except numbers. If Word sorts your numbers as text, number 1 will be followed by 10, 11, 12 and so on, and number 2 will come after 19!

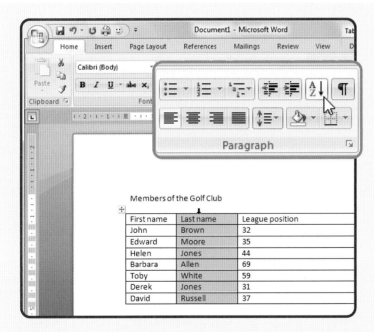

4 You can choose to sort in ascending or descending order. If you have selected more than one column, you can set the order of your sort – for instance, sorting the data first by column two, then by column three. If you have selected your column headers, click the 'Header row' option in the 'My list has' section, so that your headers don't get sorted as well. Click **OK**.

3 If you have a table of information, you can easily reorganise your columns using the Sort feature. Highlight the cells to be sorted, or highlight a whole column by positioning the insertion point at the top of the column and clicking when it changes to an arrow. Go to the 'Paragraph' group and click on the **Sort** button.

Doing a calculation

One of Word's useful features is that it offers some of the basic functions of a spreadsheet package, such as Excel. It enables you to perform calculations and you can also use formulas in many ways. You can calculate your personal expenditure, develop a table for basic bookkeeping or work out a business plan.

SEE ALSO...
- *Using tables* p48
- *Sort a list* p96

BEFORE YOU START
You will need an empty row in your table in which to put the formula's result. Position the cursor where you want the row, right-click and select **Insert**, then **Insert Rows Above**.

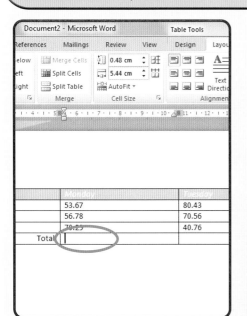

1 To create a formula to add up a column of numbers in a table, click on the empty cell below the column. Go to the **Layout** tab and click on **Formula**. The Formula dialogue box will appear on screen.

2 The 'Formula' panel displays '=SUM(ABOVE)'. This means that it is offering to add up the cells in your column. The equals (=) sign always starts a formula. 'SUM' means addition. '(ABOVE)' means that the formula applies to all the cells directly above your selected cell.
  Click **OK** to activate the formula. The total immediately appears in your table.

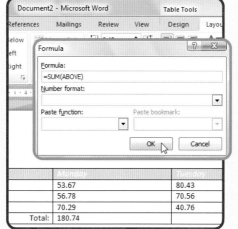

3 Alternatively, you can specify a range of cells on which to carry out a function by enclosing them in brackets in the 'Formula' panel. Cells are described using letters for columns and numbers for rows.

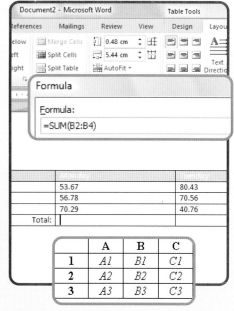

Different calculations

You can do more than simple addition in your tables. Here are some of the options available in the 'Paste function' menu (see step 5): 'SUM' is for addition, while 'MIN' finds the lowest value and 'MAX' finds the highest value. To multiply values use 'PRODUCT' and to find the number of items in a list use 'COUNT'. You can also round numbers to a specific decimal place using 'ROUND(x,y)' where 'x' is the value and 'y' is the desired number of decimal places.

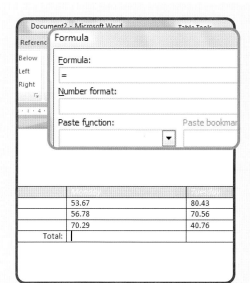

4 To use a function other than 'SUM', click in the cell where you want the result to appear. Go to the **Layout** tab and click on **Formula**. The Formula dialogue box will appear on screen again. This time delete the formula offered to you, leaving the equals sign in place.

5 Click the down arrow beside 'Paste function' to reveal a choice of functions. Scroll down and select **Average** – it will appear in the Formula panel. Now type '(ABOVE)' or type the range of cells between brackets.

You can also choose how the numbers are displayed in your table by clicking the drop-down list below 'Number format' and selecting one of the options.

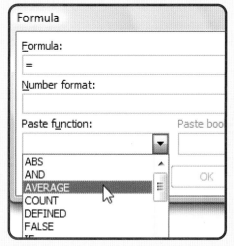

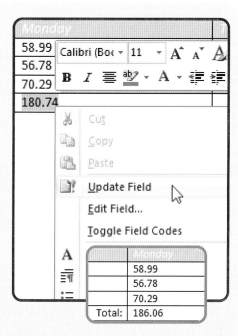

6 If you change the formula or any of the figures on which the formula is based, the result will not change until you update the formula. To do this, right-click on the formula cell and select **Update Field.**

Converting files to PDF

A PDF (Portable Document Format) file is a very popular way of distributing documents to others electronically, which a recipient can open even if they don't have the software used to create the documents. Word has an 'add-in' that lets you save documents directly into PDF format but you will need Adobe Acrobat Reader to view a PDF (this can be downloaded for free).

SEE ALSO...
● *Save your work p22*

 BEFORE YOU START
Create a new document. Go to the **Office** button and click on **New**. In the New Document dialogue box click on **Create**. Also make sure that you have an active internet connection.

INSTALLING THE SOFTWARE

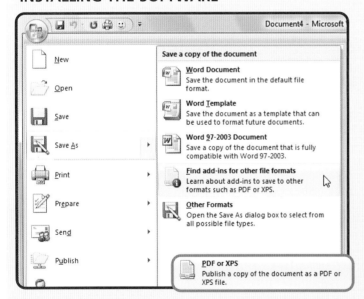

1 Type in the content of your document. To save your document as a PDF file, click on the **Office** button and then on **Save As**. If you see the option 'PDF or XPS' in the right-hand pane then the add-in has already been installed. If you can't see it in this pane, click on **Find add-ins for other file formats**.

2 The Word Help window will appear with an explanation of how to install the required add-ins. In the 'What do you want to do?' section of this window, click on the link **Install and use the Save as PDF or XPS add-in from Microsoft**.

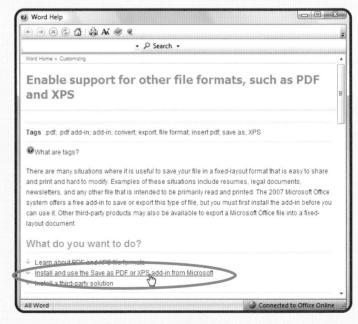

Software licences

The 'Save as PDF or XPS Add-in for 2007 Microsoft Office programs' is subject to the licence terms of Microsoft. You may not use it if you do not have a licence for the software. When prompted read the agreement and click **Continue**.

Microsoft Save as PDF or XPS Add-in for 2007 Microsoft Office programs

You must accept the Microsoft Software License Terms in order to continue the installation

PLEASE NOTE: Microsoft Corporation (or based on where you live, one of its affiliates) supplement to you. You may use a copy of this supplement with each validly licensed Office System Desktop Application software (the "software"). You may not use the sup have a license for the software. The license terms for the software apply to your use To read the license terms, go to the "Help" menu in the software. Micr the supplement as described at www.support.microsoft.com/common/

Continue

Watch out

Some of the dialogue boxes and options shown in the instructions below may differ slightly from those on your PC. This may be as a result of the options chosen while installing Windows or Office, or due to software updates received over the Net. However, this will not affect your ability to complete the project.

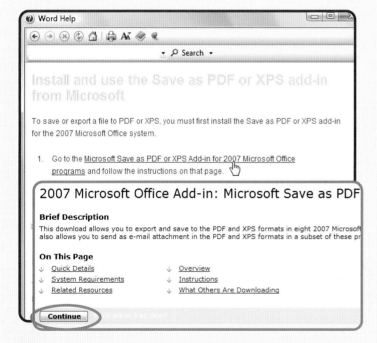

Word Help

Search

Install and use the Save as PDF or XPS add-in from Microsoft

To save or export a file to PDF or XPS, you must first install the Save as PDF or XPS add-in for the 2007 Microsoft Office system.

1. Go to the Microsoft Save as PDF or XPS Add-in for 2007 Microsoft Office programs and follow the instructions on that page.

2007 Microsoft Office Add-in: Microsoft Save as PDF

Brief Description
This download allows you to export and save to the PDF and XPS formats in eight 2007 Microsoft also allows you to send as e-mail attachment in the PDF and XPS formats in a subset of these pr

On This Page
↓ Quick Details   ↓ Overview
↓ System Requirements   ↓ Instructions
↓ Related Resources   ↓ What Others Are Downloading

Continue

3 A window called 'Install and use the Save as PDF or XPS add-in from Microsoft' will appear. Click on **Microsoft Save as PDF or** **XPS Add-in for 2007 Microsoft programs**. You will then be connected via your Web browser to the Microsoft Web site. Click on **Continue**.

4 If an Internet Explorer Security Warning dialogue box appears, click **Install**. You will now see a summary screen confirming what you are about to download. Click on **Download**. When the Download Complete dialogue box appears click on **Run**. If another Security Warning dialogue box appears, click on **Run** again. Finally, when a dialogue box displays the message 'The installation is complete', click on **OK**.

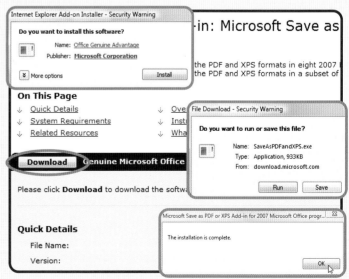

Internet Explorer Add-on Installer - Security Warning

Do you want to install this software?
Name: Office Genuine Advantage
Publisher: Microsoft Corporation

More options   Install

On This Page
↓ Quick Details   ↓ Ove
↓ System Requirements   ↓ Inst
↓ Related Resources   ↓ Wha

Download   Genuine Microsoft Office

Please click **Download** to download the softw

Quick Details
File Name:
Version:

-in: Microsoft Save as

the PDF and XPS formats in eight 2007
the PDF and XPS formats in a subset of

File Download - Security Warning

Do you want to run or save this file?
Name: SaveAsPDFandXPS.exe
Type: Application, 933KB
From: download.microsoft.com

Run   Save

Microsoft Save as PDF or XPS Add-in for 2007 Microsoft Office progr...

The installation is complete.

OK

SAVING A FILE TO PDF FORMAT

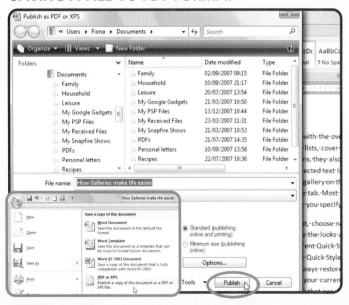

1 Open a Microsoft Office 2007 Word document and click on the **Office** button, then on **Save As** in the left pane. Select **PDF or XPS** from the options in the

right pane. In the Publish as PDF or XPS dialogue box, name your file and make sure **PDF** is selected in the 'Save as type' panel, then click on **Publish**.

2 Your newly created PDF file will be now be automatically opened in Adobe Acrobat Reader. You can now send this file to

someone, as an e-mail attachment for example, in the knowledge that they will be able to open and read it, but not alter it.

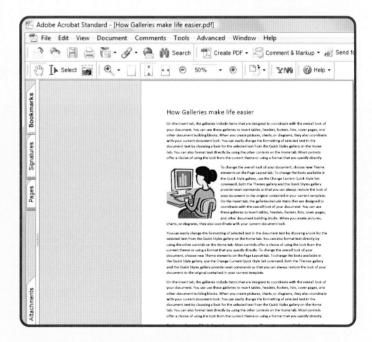

Expert advice
To publish your documents online, save them in XPS (XML Paper Specification) format. Files saved in this format can be viewed directly in a Web browser, for example Internet Explorer, without the need for a specialist reader program.

Watch out
You will now have several versions of the same document with the same name but with a different extension. Always keep the original Microsoft Word document in case you need to edit it at any time. The PDF and XPS versions of the document cannot be edited without specialist software.

How Galleries make life easier
How Galleries make life easier
How Galleries make life easier

SAVING A FILE TO XPS FORMAT

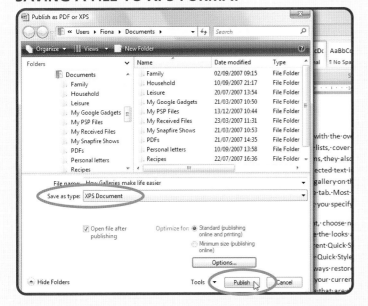

1 If you want to publish documents on the Internet, you can save them in XPS format. To do this, click on the **Office** button and then on **Save As** in the left pane. Select **PDF or XPS** in the right pane. Name your file, then click on the 'Save as type' drop-down list and select 'XPS Document'. Click on **Publish**.

2 Your document is then automatically opened in Internet Explorer if it is your default Web browser. If you use another browser, a dialogue box will appear asking what you want to do with the file. Select your browser in the 'Open with' panel and click **OK**. If the XPS file does not automatically open, close Word, locate the file and double-click on it to display it in your browser.

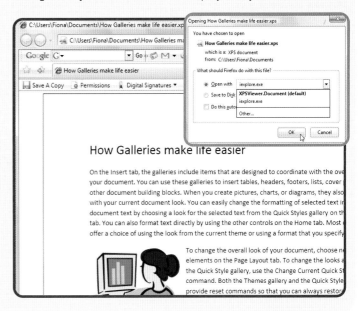

A

Active window The window in which you are working. To activate a window, click on it and it will jump in front of any other open windows on screen.

Alignment The position of text and objects on a page in relation to the margins. Text can be aligned to the left or right margin, centred down the middle of the page or justified so that lines of text fit the width of the page, column or box.

Alt key The key to the left of the spacebar on the keyboard that activates a command when pressed in combination with other keys. *See Shift key*.

Arrow keys The four keys at the bottom of the keyboard that move the insertion point up, down, left and right, or allow you to scroll through a window's contents.

AutoFormat This feature is used to apply formatting according to settings that you have created and saved.

AutoShapes A selection of predesigned graphic shapes that you insert in a document and customise to your needs.

B

Background A colour, texture or image positioned on the page as a layer on top of which all other text and objects sit.

Backspace key This is located in the top right-hand corner of the main block of letter keys on the keyboard, often showing a left-facing arrow. This key deletes text to the left of the insertion point. *See Delete key*.

Bitmap An on-screen image made up of tiny dots or 'pixels'.

Browse (in a window) To search through the contents of your computer, viewing the names of the files in each folder.

Bullet point A small graphic, often a black dot, used to indicate individual statements within a list.

Button An on-screen image on which you can click to perform a function, for example the 'OK' or 'Yes' buttons to confirm an action.

C

Caps Lock Pressing this key will cause all letters that you type to appear as capitals, or in 'upper case'. Press the key again to return to standard characters.

Cell A small, rectangular unit in a spreadsheet, database or table, into which text or figures are entered. Click on a cell to make it active.

Chart A graphic representation of data such as a graph, that can be inserted into a Word document.

Click To press and release the left mouse button once. Menu and dialogue box options and toolbar buttons are selected in this way.

Clip Another word for a ClipArt image. *See ClipArt*.

ClipArt Graphic images that come with the Word program which can be inserted into documents and then resized and manipulated.

Clipboard A virtual location where items cut or copied from a document are stored. The Word Clipboard can store several items of data at a time, regardless of size. Use the Paste command on the Clipboard Toolbar to insert a Clipboard item in a document.

Close A command to shut down the active document, but not the program. A document can be closed by clicking the 'Close' button in the top right-hand corner of a window or via the Office button.

Contextual Tabs These are additional controls that appear when a specific command has been actioned. If, for example, you are editing a table then the 'Table Tools' contextual tabs will be displayed.

Copy To make a duplicate of a file, image, or section of a document.

Cursor A marker, usually a flashing vertical line, indicating where text or inserted objects will appear. Also called the 'insertion point'.

Cursor keys *See Arrow keys*.

Cut To remove selected text and/or images to the Clipboard, where they are stored for later use.

D

Database A system for storing data so it can be easily accessed, organised, and sorted. Each entry is called a 'record' and each category in a record is called a 'field'.

Data source A file that contains information stored in database form, such as names and addresses, which can be used in a Mail Merge. *See Mail Merge*.

Default The manufacturer's settings for a program which will be used when no others have been specified by the user. For example, Word automatically checks spelling through the US dictionary. However, you can change default settings using Options in the Tools menu.

Delete To completely remove a selected file, folder or image, or a piece of text from your document.

Delete key This is located in the group of six keys to the right of the main block of letter keys on the keyboard. This key deletes text to the right of the insertion point. *See Backspace key*.

Desktop The background screen on your PC. It is the starting point for all work. Icons represent various office items, such as files, folders, and a waste basket known as the 'Recycle Bin'. The background is called 'wallpaper', while the Start button gives you access to the programs, your work and the computer's settings.

Destination document The file to which an item currently on the Clipboard is to be added. *See Source document*.

Dialogue box A window that appears on screen when you are using a program. It usually asks for preferences or further instructions to be input by the user in order to complete a procedure.

Dialogue box launcher A small arrow to the bottom right of a group on the Ribbon in Office 2007 programs that you click on to launch a dialogue box providing more options related to the group.

Digital image A picture that is stored in binary format, so it can be viewed and changed on a PC.

Document A single piece of work created in a program, also known as a 'file'.

Dots per inch (dpi) The number of dots per square inch that either make up an image on screen or that a particular printer has the capability to print. The more dots, the greater the detail and quality of the image.

Double-click To press and release the left mouse button twice in quick succession. This is most often used to open documents and folders, and to activate programs.

Drag A mouse action used to highlight text, reshape objects, or to move an object or file. Click and, keeping the left button held down, move the mouse as required.

Drop-down menu A list of options that appears when you click on one of the headings on the Menu bar.

E

Edit To make a change to an element in a document or to alter the preferences for a program.

End Pressing this key takes you to the end of the line of text on which the cursor is positioned.

Error message A small window on screen warning that a fault has occurred and, where possible, suggesting an action to remedy it.

Export To save a Word file in a form that allows it to be incorporated in another Microsoft Office application, such as PowerPoint.

External hardware Additional computer equipment attached by cable to a PC, such as a printer.

F

Field A category for information in a database, such as 'Name' or 'Address'.

File Any item stored on a computer, whether it is a program, a document, or an image.

File extension A three or four-letter code assigned to the end of the file name when it is saved. It states the type of file it is so that the computer knows in which program to open it. Common extensions are listed here:

Text	.asc .doc .html
	.msg .txt .wpd
Image	.bmp .eps .gif .jpeg
	.pict .png .tif

File format The way in which files created by different programs are saved. *See File extensions.*

Fill To apply a chosen colour to a designated area. You can also apply a mix of colours using 'Fill Effects'.

Folder An electronic storage location for keeping related files

and relevant documents together.

Font A specific style and set of characters for a typeface such as Times New Roman.

Footer A box at the base of every page of a document that contains information relevant to the whole document, such as page numbers and copyright details. *See Header.*

Format To alter a document's appearance by applying style, typography and layout options.

Form letter A correspondence, created using Mail Merge, which is used to send the same letter to many different addresses.

Formula A set of conditions that carry out a mathematical calculation.

Full Screen Reading This is the view that increases the size of the active window to fill the screen.

Function keys The 12 keys at the top of the keyboard, ranging from F1 to F12, which perform special tasks.

G

.gif file Graphics Interchange Format. A common file format for storing digital images.

Graphic Any type of digital image on a computer, including pictures, photographs and illustrations.

Group The categories into which certain tasks have been placed in Office 2007 for ease of use on the Ribbon. *See Ribbon.*

H

Handle The small squares that appear at the corners and sides of an object when you select it. They allow you to adjust the dimensions of the object by dragging them to a different position.

Header Information which appears at the top of each page of a

document.

Help key Usually the F1 key on the keyboard, this accesses advice and information on performing a task.

Highlight To select text, images or cells by dragging the cursor over the item. *See Drag.*

Home Pressing this key takes you to the start of the line of text on which the cursor is positioned.

Hyperlink A piece of underlined text or an object that you click on to take you to a specific Web page using your Web browser (provided you have access to the Internet).

Hyphen A short 'dash' used to join two words, such as that in 'right-hand'. Word also lets you use a non-breaking hyphen. This prevents a hyphenated word from being split when it appears at the end of a line by taking the whole word over to the next line.

I

Icon A graphical representation of a file or a function, designed to be easily recognisable. For example, the printer icon on the Standard toolbar accesses the print function.

Import To bring text, images or files from another program into a Word document.

Indent To position a line or lines of text further from the page margin than the following or preceding lines. Often used to mark the beginning of a new paragraph.

Inkjet printer A type of printer that works by squirting tiny drops of black or coloured ink onto the surface of the paper. Most home printers use inkjets.

Insert To add an element to a document, such as an image or text. This is best done using the Insert tab.

Insertion point *See Cursor.*

Internet Short for 'International Network'. Millions of computers worldwide linked by telephone and cable lines. Users access the Internet via a phone connection to their ISP.

ISP Internet Service Provider. A company that provides a connection for your computer to access the Internet via a telephone line.

Italic A style of writing whereby the letters are typed with a slight slant to the right. It is most often used to emphasise specific words or phrases, or for the names of books and films.

J

.jpeg Joint Photographics Experts Group. A file format that compresses the data required to make up an image so that it uses less space.

Justify To force lines of text to fit either the space between the left and right margins, or a specified column width.

K

Keyboard shortcut A combination of keys pressed simultaneously to issue a specific command.

L

Laser printer A type of printer that uses a laser to etch images onto a drum and then transfers them to paper, giving a higher quality printout than an inkjet printer.

Layout This refers to the way that items are arranged on a page.

Letterhead A design or information, such as your name and address, that appears at the top of all your letters.

Log on To access a restricted computer, file or Web site using a security procedure, like a password.

M

Macro A series of commands or actions that can be recorded, then activated by a keystroke and played back when required.

Mail Merge A way of incorporating name and address data from another application, such as the Address Book, into Word, allowing you to repeat a letter with the same content but with personalised addresses.

Margins The white space around the edge of the document, the dimensions of which can be adjusted.

Maximise To increase the size of a window so that it covers the entire Desktop area.

Minimize To reduce a window to a button on the Taskbar. This allows you to continue running several programs without cluttering the Desktop with windows you are not using at that time.

Modem A device to allow you to connect to the Internet via a telephone line.

Monitor The unit similar to a television which displays all of your work on-screen.

Mouse pointer A small arrow or cursor on screen that moves in relation to the mouse.

Multimedia Computing which combines different methods of communication such as sound, images, text, and video.

My Documents A Windows Desktop icon representing a folder for storing files created by the user.

N

Net Short for Internet. *See Internet*.

Non-printing characters These are symbols that can be viewed in the document on-screen to show word spacing, paragraphs and line returns. They do not appear on the printed document.

Normal View A simplified view used for typing, editing and formatting text. You do not see the page boundaries in this view. *See Print Layout*.

O

Object A self-contained item that can be placed in a Word document and retains its characteristics, such as an image or a spreadsheet.

Office button A button at the top left of the Office 2007 programs that gives access to some basic functions, such as print and save. It is also the route to accessing some on-line, program-specific extras such as templates.

Online The status of a computer when it is actively connected to the Internet.

Open To bring a file, folder or program into use.

Orientation An option available when creating a document. Users can choose to set up a page as either Landscape (of greater width than height) or Portrait (of greater height than width), depending on how they want the final document to appear.

P

Page break The position in a document at which one page ends and another begins. Insert a page break manually at any point you choose within a document and Word will automatically reposition all the elements that follow the new break.

Page Setup The settings that allow you to specify the layout of your page, margin sizes, paper size and how you view your document.

Page Up/Page Down These keys take you up or down respectively, to the next or previous page of your document.

Panel A space in a dialogue box in which information and text can be entered.

Paste To insert text or other data that has been cut or copied to the clipboard.

Pixels Individual dots on a computer screen. The greater the concentration of pixels, the higher the level of detail and improvement in the quality of display.

Plain Text The way of saving a text document if you want to open it in another word processor or e-mail program. However, any formatting or styling you applied will be removed.

Point size A standard scale for measuring typefaces. For example, the text on this page is 8 point, whereas newspaper headlines are often 72 point.

Pop-up menu A list of options that appears when you right-click on the Desktop.

Printer driver Software that enables the operating system to communicate with the printer.

Print Layout The document view that shows the page edges so you can see the position of text and objects as you are working. *See Full Screen Reading* and *Web Layout*.

Print Preview The on-screen display of how a document will look when it is printed. Changes cannot be made to the document when using Print Preview, as it is for visual reference only.

Properties The attributes of a file or folder, such as the date it was originally created, the format and the author's name.

Q

Quick Access Toolbar A customisable toolbar that contains commands independent of the tab that is currently displayed.

R

Radio button A small circle beside an option which you click to activate. An activated option will have a black dot in the radio button.

Range A group of related cells in a table or spreadsheet.

Recycle Bin A Desktop icon and feature used to store files ready for permanent deletion. To delete files in the Recycle Bin, right-click on the Recycle Bin icon and select 'Empty Recycle Bin' from the menu.

Resize To adjust the dimensions of an object in a Word document. Do this by clicking and dragging the handles that appear on its edges when you select the object.

Resolution The degree of detail on a screen or a printed document, measured in dots per inch (dpi). The higher the dpi, the better the detail.

Return key The large key on the right-hand side of the main block of letter keys on the keyboard. Press to create a new paragraph in your text.

Ribbon A new toolbar-focused way of working in Office 2007. Clicking on the tabs at the top of the ribbon gives easy access to a number of associated tasks, collected in groups for a more intuitive approach.

Rich Text Format A way of saving a document so that if it is opened in another word processor or Microsoft program, it will retain the formatting and styling that you applied to it.

Right-click To press and release the right mouse button once. In Word, this causes a pop-up menu of options to appear with different options depending on the item on which you clicked.

S

Save To store or copy a document to a disk, most often a floppy or the hard disk.

Save As This function allows you to allocate a name to a file you are saving. It also lets you save an existing file to a different drive or in an alternative format without affecting the original saved file.

Scroll To move through the contents of a window or menu vertically or horizontally.

Scroll bar The grey panel running either down the right-hand side or along the bottom of a window containing a darker grey block. By clicking on the block and dragging along the panel you can scroll down the page or from side to side at a quick speed.

Search A mini-program that searches for a file, usually by its name or creation date. Also, a command which searches a document for specific information, such as a word or phrase.

Select To click on a file, folder, image, text, or other item, so it can be moved or manipulated.

Server A computer that is the main file storage location connected to a network of other computers.

Shift key Used to type a capital letter when pressed at the same time as a letter key, or to type the symbols on the number keys. It can give you access to program functions when pressed together with other keys. For example, by pressing 'Shift' + 'Alt' + 'T' it is possible to insert the current time in your document.

Software Programs designed to perform specific functions. Word is an example of software designed for word-processing.

Source document The file from which an item is cut or copied to the Clipboard for use in another document.
See Destination document.

Spacebar The wide key along the bottom of the keyboard for inserting spaces between words.

Spellcheck Checks your spelling and suggests corrections. It can use alternative dictionaries to which you can also add terms.

Standard toolbar The line of small icons in Word that sits at the top of the window below the Menu bar and contains common features used when creating word processing documents. These include Save, Print, Spelling and Grammar checker, and Cut, Copy and Paste.

Start The button on the left of the Taskbar for viewing the Start menu.

Status bar The grey bar along the bottom of program windows containing information about the current document.

Style The appearance of the various elements of a document.
See Format.

T

Tab(1) Short for 'tabulate'. A feature for positioning text at various distances from the left margin.

Tab(2) Used to access commands held in logical groups on the Ribbon. *See Ribbon.*

Tab key The key to the left of the 'Q' key, used to position text at preset intervals across the page. It is also used to move between cells in spreadsheets, or to move from one database field to the next.

Table A group of cells in rows and columns, in which you can type text or place images. Inserting a table in a Word document helps to arrange the elements neatly on the page.

Taskbar The bar usually positioned along the bottom of the screen that displays the Start button, and buttons for programs and documents that are already open or in use.

Task Pane A window next to your document displaying your current task options.

Template A format for saving a document so that its elements can be used to create similar documents.

Themes Background styles that you can apply to your document. Themes can only be printed out as a watermark effect, rather than as a solid image.

Thesaurus An alphabetical list of words and their possible synonyms or antonyms arranged similar to a standard dictionary.

Track changes A feature which lets other people add comments to your document without actually making permanent alterations.

Truetype A fonts file that permits characters to have smooth edges no matter how small or large they appear in a document.

Typeface *See Font.*

U

Undo A function that allows you to reverse the last task or several tasks that you carried out.

V

View A menu of options which allows you to change the way a document is displayed on screen.

W

Watermark A feature that adds an image or text, so that it prints as a faint background effect behind the text in a document, thus giving the effect of a stationery watermark.

Web Layout Lets you see how documents would look if viewed in a browser. *See Full Screen Reading* and *Print Layout.*

Window The self-contained viewing and work area of a file or program. Several windows can be open at once on the Desktop.

Windows Explorer A program for viewing the contents of a computer in a single window.

Wizard A program tool that guides users through customising a predesigned document.

WordArt Text created in a graphic form that can be customised and imported into a document for decorative effect.

Word processing Text-based activites on the computer, such as letter writing. Word processing allows you to create professionally styled documents using a wide range of fonts, sizes and colours.

Wrapping The manner in which an object, such as an image, is positioned in relation to text. It can sit behind the text or make the text flow around it in various ways.

Z

Zoom To enlarge an area of a document for ease of viewing.

INDEX

Numbers shown in **bold** type are for main references to the subject listed

How to do just about anything in Microsoft® Word – Office 2007

was edited and designed by The Reader's Digest Association Limited, London

First edition copyright © 2008
The Reader's Digest Association Limited,
11 Westferry Circus, Canary Wharf, London E14 4HE.
www.readersdigest.co.uk

We are committed both to the quality of our products and the service we provide to our customers. We value your comments, so please do contact us on **08705 113366**, or via our Web site at **www.readersdigest.co.uk**
If you have any comments or suggestions about this book, e-mail us at **gbeditorial@readersdigest.co.uk**

Origination: Colour Systems Limited, London

Printed and bound in China

Book code 400-368 UP0000-1
ISBN 978 0 276 44264 3
Oracle code 250011973H.00.24